JUNG & REICH: THE BODY AS SHADOW

John P. Conger

North Atlantic Books
Berkeley, California

Jung and Reich: The Body as Shadow
Copyright © 1988 by John P. Conger

ISBN 01-55643-037-X (paperback)
ISBN 01-55643-038-8 (cloth)

Publisher's address:
North Atlantic Books
2800 Woolsey Street
Berkeley, California 94705

Cover art from the Rosarium philosophorum, secunda pars alchimiae de lapide
philosophico (Frankfurt, 1550)
Cover and book design by Paula Morrison
Typeset in Palatino by Paul Weisser

Jung and Reich: The Body as Shadow is sponsored by the Society for the Study of
Native Arts and Sciences, a nonprofit educational corporation whose goals are
to develop an ecological and crosscultural perspective linking various scientific,
social, and artistic fields; to nurture a holistic view of arts, sciences, humanities,
and healing; and to publish and distribute literature on the relationship of mind,
body, and nature.

Library of Congress Cataloging-in-Publication Data

Conger, John P., 1935-
    Jung and Reich.

    Bibliography: p.
    Includes index.
    1. Psychoanalysis. 2. Jung, C. G. (Carl Gustav), 1875-1961. 3. Reich,
Wilhelm, 1897-1957. 4. Mind and body. I. Title.
BF173.C5465 1988   150.19′5′0922   88-31251
ISBN 1-55643-038-8
ISBN 1-55643-037-X (pbk.)

To Jane, a divine twin, who wrestled with me,
seeking out the integrity of body and soul.

Contents

Preface

One day I had a fantasy about Wilhelm Reich and Carl Jung. What, I wondered, might these two men, who never actually met or corresponded, have been able to give each other if they had had a long and deep association? My thoughts ran to therapy. What if they had been in therapy with *each other*? What could they have learned? The ideas that followed became the inspiration for this book.

Acknowledgments

I wish to acknowledge the great encouragement and critical assistance of my friends Bill Schlansky, Nancy Laleau, and Craig Comstock, and the skillful and painstaking collaboration of my editor, Paul Weisser.

To Wendy Davis Larkin, I extend my warmest thanks for the many hours she spent typing my manuscript and supporting me through the shadowy periods of the work.

I am also grateful for and honored by the bioenergetic training and influence of Alexander Lowen, whose careful criticism of my text was invaluable.

Finally, I am deeply indebted to David Boadella for his astute reading of my manuscript and to Myron Sharaf for his insight, his scholarship, his humanity, and his enduring friendship.

Chapter 1

The Foundations of Human Nature

> To darkness are they doomed who worship only the body
> and to greater darkness they who worship only the spirit. . . .
> They who worship both the body and the spirit, by the body
> overcome death, and by the spirit achieve immortality.
>
> —*The Upanishads*

An Anglo-Saxon writer commented that life is like the bird that flies into the mead hall and for a few moments is warmed by the fire, only to fly out again into the darkness. In so brief a time, it is difficult for any single thinker to work through the formidable tasks he assigns himself. Our lives have about them a ruthless internal economy, so that we are driven through time by our daemon, and not always given time to reflect.

It would be foolish for psychologists to feel that they had discovered the human psyche. The spiritual disciplines and world literature have studied the psyche for thousands of years. It may be our unmistakable failing that each of us rediscovers the wheel for himself (or herself). Psychology provides a conscious meeting point—as Heidegger says, a clearing in the forest of being—to observe man's relationship to his environment and to the legion he calls himself.

Modern psychology has experienced only a brief career, having piggybacked its way from the mind of one great thinker to another, from Freud to the resolute children he struggled with to keep from leaving home. "I am the teacher of athletes," wrote

Walt Whitman. "He that by me spreads a wider breast than my own proves the width of my own. He most honors my style who learns under it to destroy the teacher."[1] Unlike Whitman, unfortunately, Freud could not allow his peers or his followers to outdistance him. One by one, the great ones left Freud, troubled, angry, in conflict over the terrible loss of friendship and approval; the legacy of isolation, contentiousness, and superiority remained with them. But now more than eighty years have passed since *The Interpretation of Dreams*, and we can turn again to see if these men were in fact describing separate realities or reached into the experience of human nature common to us all.

There is a tendency in psychology to embrace one system and to isolate oneself from the wealth of learning, to split off as if each theoretician had hold of a different part of the elephant. But it may just be that, after all these years, we have stumbled into a larger vision encompassing more than the knowledge derived from holding the trunk or a leg. Two such theoreticians who would appear to have hold of entirely different elephants were Carl Jung and Wilhelm Reich.

Carl Gustav Jung was born on July 26, 1875, in Kesswil, Switzerland. As a youth, he was interested in theology, archaeology, folktales, and occult phenomena. He studied medicine at the University of Basel, and decided to study psychiatry after reading Krafft-Ebing. He began work under Eugen Bleuler at the Burghölzli Psychiatric Clinic in Zurich in 1900, and also studied with Pierre Janet at the Salpêtrière in Paris in 1902. In 1903, he married Emma Rauschenbach, with whom he also collaborated until her death in 1955.

Jung met Freud in 1906, but although each was powerfully affected by the other, their profound disagreements prevented a long-term association. Their friendship was severed in 1913 after Jung published *Symbols of Transformation*.[2] During this period, Jung had become increasingly interested in the unconscious images present in mythology, and resigned from the clinic in 1909 to pursue his private practice and research.

He traveled a great deal during the 1920s, but in 1922 he purchased a tract of land in Bollingen, on Lake Zurich, where he began to construct and continually modify a stone castle he called The Tower. His private practice, research, and publication remained prolific through the 1940s.

In 1944, Jung suffered a heart attack, and in 1947 he retired to the Bollingen Tower. His study of the unconscious continued unabated, however; and in 1958 he published his autobiography, *Memories, Dreams, Reflections*.[3] He died on June 6, 1961, after a brief illness.

Wilhelm Reich was born in Dobrzcynica, Galicia, on March 24, 1897. He spent his childhood on the family farm. After service in the Austrian army during World War I, he studied medicine in Vienna, married a fellow medical student, and began work in the Julius Wagner-Jauregg Psychiatric Clinic. Later, as an assistant in Freud's Psychoanalytic Polyclinic, he was admitted to the inner circle of Freud's close associates. In 1927, *The Function of the Orgasm* was published, followed in 1933 by *Character Analysis* and *The Mass Psychology of Fascism*.[4]

Reich was an active member of the Austrian Socialist Party and then of the Communist Party. His political activity, along with his departure from psychoanalytic orthodoxy regarding sexuality, caused a break with Freud. This combination of stigmata, compounded later by scientifically questionable research into orgone energy, was responsible for the dissolution of his family life and for hostile reactions to his work throughout Europe and the United States.

Reich emigrated to America in 1939, remarried, settled in Rangely, Maine, and continued to study orgone energy. Since he was not licensed to practice medicine in the United States, his orgone therapy came under the scrutiny of the Food and Drug Administration, and he was eventually sentenced to a two-year prison term. He died in Lewisburg Penitentiary on November 3, 1957.

Some people are offended by Reich, and others are offended by Jung. Those who are offended by Reich are most bothered by his emphasis on genitality and his claims concerning orgone. People are offended by Jung because of his "mysticism," his psychological investigations of spiritual disciplines and experience.

People are often offended by the knowledge they need most. We resist our deepest education. Most Jungians would profit by a bath of Reich, and most Reichians by immersion in Jung. While we seek agreement, protection, and security, our best path may be toward discomfort.

A new client once informed me that counseling had failed her but that she needed Bioenergetics. However, she was offended when I mentioned Jung. She was militantly against Jung, and yet the very area she was most cut off from was a conscious, verbalized awareness of meaning in her life and experiences, and her unconscious foundations. She made it clear that her path toward a sense of connectedness and meaning, if it were to be traveled at all, must be more unconsciously engaged through the metaphor of the body and the body experience. For this client, and others like her, the insistence on her chosen form of treatment reinforced many of her troubling defenses and limited her access to deeper healing and wholeness. Jung and Reich were brilliant theoreticians, and their *combined* models of healing have much to offer us.

Jung was fascinated with questions of religion and archaeology. Although rigorous within a European scientific tradition, he was guided by the north star of his alchemical dreams. Armed with the shield of empiricism and a theory of knowledge derived from Immanuel Kant, he entered an unconscious world larger than his personal one, an unconscious world represented by myth, allegory, and fairy tale. In particular, he was drawn to study the Gnostics and later the alchemists.

Jung's great gift was that he was able to translate the spiritual experience that had been entirely in the province of religious systems into the language of psychology, where it could be questioned and examined. He was able to translate the myths of other times and cultures into our twentieth-century myth of science, to teach us techniques to engage the unconscious in our journey home.

There are two major aspects to Wilhelm Reich. The most apparent in the younger Reich was an extraordinary concreteness in his thinking and a somewhat humorless nature. He was also obsessive, brilliant, enormously energetic, extroverted, organizational, combative, competitive, and one who appeared to follow the scientific tradition, which he presented as concrete, objective, rational, and tangible. In his early career, he was a militant atheist who held religion accountable for participating in the development of the mass character in man, the fertile ground for fascism.

Present throughout his life, but more apparent in his later years, was a more fluid and intuitive nature. With the discovery of orgone energy, he stepped from the stage of urban life into "the meadow," into nature, where, more isolated, still clothed tightly with the cloak of science, he became more a seer, a prophet. He was able to see and understand in his heart what many of the great artists and poets and spiritual teachers have seen, and found himself related to the world of nature. "No great poet or writer, no great thinker or artist," Reich said, "has ever escaped from this deep and ultimate awareness of being somehow and somewhere rooted in nature at large."[5]

Reich attempted to tie into something fundamental in nature, to ground in nature. He sought what he called a common functioning principle, an underlying similarity among differences. With the great awareness he achieved in the last ten years of his life, standing on the ragged edge of his own sanity, sometimes seeing what others did not see, accused of insanity and viciously attacked, Reich finally could acknowledge that he saw what Jung saw.

Of course, the larger ocean that Jung had sailed upon so many years earlier, which he called the collective unconscious, was mystically discovered—and so, Reich concluded, had quite rightly been dismissed by Freud. But Reich had come upon the cosmic orgone energy ocean as a scientist and could scientifically prove its existence with a Geiger counter.[6] Jung translated the spiritual journey into the more neutral terminology of psychology. Reich explored the nature of genuine contact, pleasure, and affirmation of life without having to establish it in a belief system.

Both Jung and Reich returned man to himself and to his inner process. Both understood that the kingdom is within and that man too easily gives himself away. Both have been considered "crazy" or "mystics" for speaking about the inexhaustible abundance that has backed the fragile, tenacious human experiment from the dawn of time.

Coming from different directions and in different styles, Jung and Reich both stepped through the layers of personality, the *shadow* and *character defense*, the *secondary layer* and *personal unconscious*, to experience the wider collective world of nature, which has its own functional logic. From their rigid particularity, they both stepped into an experience where, as Jung says, "Man is no longer a distinct individual, but his mind widens out and merges into the mind of mankind—not the conscious mind but the unconscious mind of mankind where we are all the same."[7]

The psychological systems of both Reich and Jung took them "down to the very foundations of life" so wonderfully expressed in the *I Ching*, Hexagram 48, "The Well":

> We must go down to the very foundations of life. For any merely superficial ordering of life that leaves its deepest needs unsatisfied is as ineffectual as if no attempt at order had ever been made. . . .
>
> However men may differ in disposition and in education, the foundations of human nature are the same in everyone. And every human being can draw in the course of his education from the inexhaustible well-spring of the divine in man's nature.[8]

Like the life of man, the inexhaustible well remains the same, abundant to all, even as nations change and generations give birth and die.

Notes

1. Walt Whitman, "Song of Myself," no. 47, in *Leaves of Grass* (New York: New American Library, 1958), p. 92.

2. C. G. Jung, *Symbols of Transformation: An Analysis of the Prelude to a Case of Schizophrenia*, 2nd ed., trans. R. F. C. Hull, Bollingen Series XX, vol. 5 (Princeton: Princeton University Press, 1956).

3. C. G. Jung, *Memories, Dreams, Reflections*, revised edition, trans. Richard and Clara Winston, ed. Aniela Jaffé (New York: Pantheon, 1973).

4. Wilhelm Reich, *The Function of the Orgasm*, trans. Theodore P. Wolfe (New York: Meridian, 1970); idem, *Character Analysis*, 3rd ed., trans. Theodore P. Wolfe (New York: Farrar, Straus & Giroux, 1949); idem, *The Mass Psychology of Fascism*, trans. Vincent R. Carfagno (New York: Farrar, Straus & Giroux, 1970).

5. Wilhelm Reich, *Cosmic Superimposition*, trans. Mary Boyd Higgins and Therese Pol (New York: Farrar, Straus & Giroux, 1973), p. 280.

6. Wilhelm Reich, *Reich Speaks of Freud* (New York: Farrar, Straus & Giroux, 1967), pp. 88–89.

7. C. G. Jung, *Analytical Psychology: Its Theory and Practice* (New York: Vintage, 1968), p. 46.

8. *The I Ching or Book of Changes*, trans. Richard Wilhelm and Cary F. Baynes, Bollingen Series XIX (Princeton: Princeton University Press, 1967), p. 48.

Chapter 2

Jung and Reich: An Overview of Similarities and Differences

With full gaze the animal sees the open.
Only our eyes, as if reversed, are like snares
set around it, block the freedom of its going.
Only from the face of the beast do we know
what is outside; for even little children
we turn around and force them to look backward
at the world of forms, and they do not see the open
so deep in the animal's eyes. Free from death.
Only we see that; but the beast is free
and has its death always behind it and God before it,
and when it walks it goes toward eternity,
as springs flow. Never, not for a single day
do we have pure space before us in which the flowers
are always unfolding.

—Rainer Maria Rilke, *The Duino Elegies*

A study of Jung and Reich, their theories and their personal journeys, their similarities and differences, provides us with a way of exploring ourselves and an opportunity to understand our embodiment, the fuller range of our spiritual and sexual lives. This chapter outlines a number of similarities and differences before plunging into a more detailed investigation. In the first half of this book, the lives and significant concepts of Reich and Jung are discussed in preparation for the comparisons of the later chapters.

In some ways, Jung and Reich were very different. Reich was extroverted, a sensation type in Jung's typology, caught in the polarity of sensation-intuition. Jung was introverted, predominantly mental, and his feeling nature was in polarity. Reich was idealistic, romantic, intellectually concrete, complex and brilliant, focused with a restricted sense of humor, very much gripped with a seriousness and social optimism that C. P. Snow has noted in some scientists.[1] Jung was abstract, allegorical, multifaceted, direct, mythic, with a great sense of humor. Reich alienated his followers. Jung maintained a permanent, loyal community. Reich was dispossessed, a citizen of the world. Jung was firmly rooted in Switzerland. Reich, as he grew older, became fascinated with Jesus, whom he saw as a prototype of the unarmored natural man. Jung, raised in a restrictive, unreflective Christianity, learned from the study of Hermes. Reich believed that evil was a secondary result of blocked energy and that the core of man was simple, direct, and loving. Jung felt that evil went to the very depths of the psyche and was present in the image of God. Reich felt that libido was a measurable sexual energy, which he later extended to what he called the orgone ocean, the energy of the universe. Jung felt that sexual energy was only one aspect of libido.

On the surface, Jung and Reich appear to have been utterly different in their natures and in their fields of interest. In general, Reich is seen as the one who sought to heal the mind/body split through greater attention to the body and, in particular, to the bioenergetic function of sexuality. Jung is recognized as one who sought to heal the split in the psyche of modern man that divorces him from his roots, from the archetypes, from his soul, through an encompassing psychological integration involving a symbolic process.

But as we study Jung and Reich further, we discover that Jung was also deeply concerned with the relation of matter and psyche, energy and the body; and Reich, as he grew older, concerned himself increasingly with spiritual matters and a sense of rootedness in nature. One appeared to take the high road of spirit, and the other the low road of the body, but both managed to meet in a number of unexpected places. Their adventures, their passionate

10

and fascinating journeys into the nature of our existence in body and psyche, raise questions for us all.

It is hard for us to know how to think about our embodied selves. Are we simply *in* our bodies, or are we embodied and only imagine we are *in* our bodies? Are we bodies that imagine all sorts of unreal fantasies? We know what it is like to drive mindlessly in our cars, apparently deeply absorbed someplace else. Suddenly, our turn off the freeway draws us to attention. We land back in our bodies with a harsh jolt. Were we really out of our bodies? As we become engrossed in a telephone conversation, our environment dissolves. Where are we? At an equidistant point? With such familiar experiences, we are legitimately bewildered when called upon to explain what *really* happens, because our consciousness as well as our embodied lives are a mystery to us. And let us suppose that we are *out* of our bodies. How does psychic energy work? Is it a bioelectrical energy that is measurable? Jung puzzled over the nature of psychic energy, which he called libido, accepting Freud's terminology. He saw that Freud's psychological system was a closed energy system in which thoughts repressed in the unconscious would appear in some other form. He saw that symbols bound and released energy, but he found no scientific way to validate the physical nature of psychic energy. In 1952, in an essay on synchronicity, Jung described parapsychological phenomena investigated in England by J. B. Rhine. In his conclusion, he describes the "out-of-body" experiences of a woman who appeared to have died in her hospital bed, only to recover and recount vividly an out-of-body experience that gave her conscious access to all the happenings around her apparent death, which she "saw" and "heard" from a point as if on the ceiling. Jung wonders if there is "some other nervous substrata in us, apart from the cerebrum, that can think and perceive, or whether the psychic processes that go on in us during loss of consciousness are synchronistic phenomena, i.e., events which have no causal connection with organic processes."[2]

Reich was convinced that sexual energy, libido, empowered the psyche and that the libido was measurable.

Other questions around our sexual and spiritual natures are raised by the study of Reich and Jung. Our sexual functioning is a sensitive barometer of our emotional state. Was Reich right when he concluded that neurotic adjustment was sustained by unreleased sexual energy? Critical and basic questions concerning the elementary issues of our nature are unresolved. While spiritual concerns have, at times, been explained away by biological reductionistic thought, Jung argued that images of God are certainly in the unconscious mind of each of us. In his practice, he did not seek to determine whether God existed outside the images of the unconscious. We unconsciously deify something: ourselves, reason, science, sexuality, our ancestors, perhaps. And to those spiritually minded persons who ignore the body, considering it as insignificant as a change of clothes, Reich has a point to consider. The body does not lie to those who can read its message. Rages and sorrows, tears and agonies are frozen history in the contracted musculature that unconsciously conditions our life and feeling. We may desperately try to transcend the body because we cannot release the burden held in the bodily armor.

In reality, the similarities between Jung and Reich far outnumber the short list of differences already discussed. In the remaining portion of this chapter, a number of similarities will be listed and briefly explored. Some similarities will have profound implications, and others, more personal, may seem to be mere curiosities. What possible significance can we attribute to the rages of Reich and Jung? It has been important to me to explore their personal natures, providing earth around their theoretical roots.

Similarities

- Both men went down to the foundations of life.
- Both felt that mind and body are different aspects of the same thing.
- Both felt that nature uses man to know itself.
- Both were alchemists.
- Both added something to the exploration of the masculine and feminine in relationship.
- Both theorized about evil and the role of the devil.
- Both were at war with traditional religion.
- Both felt that the culture was pathological and that normality is not sanity. Like Nietzsche, both

were critical of the mass man.

- Both were criticized for disturbing traditional science with their inclusive methods. Both sought to translate mystical experiences into the language of science.
- Both developed nonverbal ways of working with the psyche that they felt evoked the deepest expressions of self. Reich worked with energy and the body, and Jung with images and symbols of the psyche.
- Both believed that patients need to face their therapists and talk directly with them rather than employing Freud's couch method.
- Both painted pictures as a way of grasping their inner experiences more directly.
- Both built houses to realize their visions externally.
- Both were powerful prose writers.
- Both were not only theoreticians but also gifted therapists and teachers.
- Both had breakdowns following their breaks with Freud.
- Both were interested in UFOs. Reich felt that they were objectively real, whereas Jung saw them as projected symbols of the self.
- Both wrote controversial books that were personal expressions not originally intended for publication: Reich's *Listen, Little Man!* and Jung's *The Answer to Job.*
- Both believed that work should determine one's say in a community.
- Both were interested in the electrical charge of the skin and the effect of emotions on the charge.
- Both took pride in being in the military.
- Both came from parents who were unhappy in their marriage, and both had one other sibling.
- Both had eczema as children.
- Both suffered from tachycardia (rapid heart action) in later years and had heart attacks.

- Both erupted unexpectedly into rages in their later years.

Let us consider each of these points at greater length.

Both went down to the foundations of life. Both Jung and Reich reached that level where timely, cultural, and individual differences no longer distract us from the vast, inexhaustible life we share in common. Jung found language for this lifelong experience in the concept of the collective unconscious. Reich, by his commitment to the study of nature, through his attention to the natural uninhibited functions of the body, saw the body of man reconnected to the expansion and contraction of all living things. Reich felt rooted in nature as a part of the cosmic orgone ocean.

Both felt that mind and body are different aspects of the same thing. Reich, of course, boldly proclaimed the functional identity of the psyche and the body. "Psyche and somata," he wrote, "are two parallel processes in mutual interaction: *psychophysical parallelism.*"[3]

While Reich worked with the body to reintegrate it with the psyche of man, Jung saw the body and spirit as mere aspects of the only reality we can truly lay claim to, the psyche:

> Body and spirit are to me mere aspects of the reality of the psyche. Psychic experience is the only immediate experience. Body is as metaphysical as spirit. Ask the modern physicist what body is, they are coming fast across to the recognition of the reality of the psyche.[4]

Both felt that nature uses man to know itself. Man is nature's extension of itself, to know itself; and Reich, in his later years, reflected upon the cosmic orgone ocean and man's function and place in nature. In *Cosmic Superimposition*, he wrote: "Thus in an ultimate sense, in self-awareness and in striving for the perfection of knowledge and full integration of one's biofunctions, *the cosmic orgone energy becomes aware of itself.*"[5]

Jung described an experience he had in Africa that filled him with faith concerning man's evolution to a higher consciousness and confirmed for him the purpose of nature to know itself:

> "But why on earth," you may ask, "should it be necessary for man to achieve, by hook or by crook, a higher level of consciousness?" This is truly the crucial question, and I do not find the answer easy. Instead of a real answer, I can only make a confession of faith: I believe that, after thousands and millions of years, someone had to realize that this wonderful world of mountains and oceans, suns and moons, galaxies and nebulae, plants and animals, *exists*.[6]

Both were alchemists. Jung, in devoting years to his study of alchemy, established it as a process parallel to his own individuation process. His tower in Bollingen, where he often retired, was designed so that someone from an earlier century would not find much that was unfamiliar. His connection with alchemy was immediate and physical as he chipped symbols into stone. Like Reich, he utilized the power of a nonverbal process.

Reich was an alchemist in an unconscious way. Boiling earth in retorts, he was fascinated by physical phenomena; and in that way, he was remarkably similar to the original alchemists. For them, matter was a great mystery, and therefore they were able to project the unconscious unwittingly upon it. Through the years, Reich's scientific advances paralleled an intense development of his spiritual awareness. He could finally understand what religious people sought after and felt; and he could finally feel connected to nature because he saw that all of life was sustained by the cosmic orgone ocean.

Both added something to the exploration of the masculine and feminine in relationship. Reich, by his exploration of the genital embrace, unmasked the false masculinity built on fear, sadistic imagery, or performance. Reich felt that all neurosis was reflected in the quality of lovemaking. Men who appear to be great lovers because they can make love all night may, in fact, not be able to find release and satisfaction. Some men are not able to let down, to let go in genital surrender, to accept a more "feminine" softness and allow themselves to "melt" in the embrace. Reich broke down the facade and armoring that prevents genuine contact. It has also been reported that, like many others of his age, he was prejudiced against homosexuals, which can reflect some confusion and fear concerning the masculine and feminine.

Jung, by his willingness to address the contrasexual in himself, the anima or animus, helped to establish the awareness of our bisexual nature and our propensity to project out the anima or animus onto a partner. By owning one's own projections, one can begin to relate to a person independent of those projections.

Both theorized about evil and the role of the devil. Reich believed that man, at his core, seeks life in a healthy, self-regulated, matter-of-fact, good-natured way. He may express anger and self-interest, but his anger and self-interest are not evil. Reich did not believe with Freud that at man's core the death instinct prevails. Evil, the devil, the death instinct, arises as a secondary reaction when natural expansive love is thwarted. Only then does an armoring process begin that deflects genital contact with others:

> The "devil" meant the absolute "evil," personified in the well-known creation of hell in Christian thinking so splendidly embodied in Goethe's Mephistopheles. Man has felt the "devil" as tempting. Why, we must ask, did he not think of God as "tempting"? If the devil represents distorted nature and God is primal, true nature, why does man feel so much more drawn to the devil than to God. . . ?
>
> The answer is, again, *the devil is tempting and so easy to follow because it represents the secondary drives that are so accessible. God is so boring and distant because it represents the core of life that has been made inaccessible by the armoring.*[7]

Jung felt that man is a representative microcosm, and that at our root there is an inseparable mix of good and evil. Humankind, built on the play of opposites, has a predisposition to deny the shadow and project it onto others. Unfortunately, in Christianity, Jesus and the Devil have been radically split apart. For that reason, Jung preferred figures such as Hermes (Mercurius) as mediators, because they represent symbols that are equally at home in darkness and in light. He was more fascinated by the figure of Mephistopheles in Goethe's *Faust* than in Faust himself.

Both were at war with traditional religion. In *The Mass Psy-*

chology of Fascism, Reich saw religious fervor as disowned and distorted sexual feeling, and he blamed the Church for creating submissive people by attacking and repressing sexual expression. In the 1950s, Reich finally became aware of what the religious people had been in touch with, and, while he still opposed a mysticism in which life is postponed for an imaginary world of reward beyond, he became reconciled to the religious mind that perceives God as a present reality. Reich had determined that same spiritual presence scientifically as the orgone energy ocean.

Jung was brought up in a rigid sectarian training by his father, a minister who had lost his faith. Jung saw the great danger of a traditional religion that denies the shadow and promises salvation by virtue of membership alone. Plagued also by dreams and visions that demanded profound understanding of spiritual processes, Jung was drawn to study the Gnostics (heretics persecuted by the early Church for doctrinal differences), because they seemed to have some understanding of the problems of integrating the dark side. Later, in his study of alchemy, Jung found substantiation for his individuation process. He communicated with many of the clergy, some of whom were upset by his writing. A few, such as the Jesuit Father Victor White, became personal friends. *The Answer to Job* expressed some of Jung's Gnostic viewpoints.

Both felt that the culture was pathological and that normality is not sanity. In his early work, Reich was struck by the vast numbers of people with neurotic structures. His observations eventually became codified in his indictment of the mass man, who was taught submission and genital weakness by the authoritarian family and the Church and was therefore easily led by a fascist leader. Reich published his ideas in *The Mass Psychology of Fascism*:

> The man reared under and bound by authority has no knowledge of the natural law of self-regulation; he has no confidence in himself. He is afraid of his sexuality because he never learned to live naturally. Thus, he declines all responsibility for his acts and decisions, and he demands direction and guidance.[8]

The man whose natural, healthy behavior has been suppressed and overrun must emotionally limp along as best he can,

17

suffering from "emotional plague." Reich wrote that "the energy which nourishes the emotional plague reactions regularly derives from genital frustration."[9] The only hope, then, was to undergo Reich's therapy, which was able to break through the neurotic character and reestablish a natural, self-regulatory person whose sexual functioning was restored.

Jung was deeply influenced by Nietzsche, and felt that any group naturally evokes a collective energy that sweeps people along unconsciously. Only through an individuation process in which a person becomes conscious of the myths or the archetypes expressed through him can such a person approach a level of real sanity. To differentiate ourselves from all the collective factors with which we identify is not to discard them but to become neutral and less driven by unconscious forces.

Both were criticized for disturbing traditional science with inclusive methods that spilled over into other fields of thought. They both felt uncomfortable with the process. Reich wrote of his experience:

> There was always too much going on in the workshop; too many facts, new causal connections, corrections of dated and inaccurate viewpoints, connections with various branches of specialized research in the natural sciences. Hence, I often had to defend myself against the criticism that I had overstepped scientific limits, that I had undertaken "too much at one time." I did not undertake too much at a time, and I did not overreach myself scientifically. No one has felt this charge of "too much" more painfully than I have. I did not set out to trace the facts; the facts and interrelations flowed toward me in superabundance. I had trouble treating them with due attention and putting them in good order. Many, many facts of great significance were lost that way; others remained uncomprehended."[10]

Jung also expressed his discomfort and sense of how unwittingly he had been thrust into a profusion of fields for which he was ill-equipped:

> The problems of analytical psychology, as I have tried to outline them here, led to conclusions that astonished even me. I fancied I

18

was working along the best scientific lines, establishing facts, observing, classifying, describing causal and functional relations, only to discover in the end that I had involved myself in a net of reflections which extend far beyond natural science and ramify into the field of philosophy, theology, comparative religion, and the humane sciences in general. This transgression, as inevitable as it was suspect, has caused me no little worry. Quite apart from my personal incompetence in these fields, it seemed to me that my reflections were suspect also in principle, because I am profoundly convinced that the "personal equation" has a telling effect upon the results of psychological observation. The tragic thing is that psychology has no self-consistent mathematics at its disposal, but only a calculus of subjective prejudices.[11]

Both developed nonverbal ways of working with the psyche that they felt evoked the deepest expressions of self. Reich worked with the body, and Jung with images and symbols of the psyche. Reich, as he grew older, preferred to watch the energy flow of the body, occasionally utilizing mechanical pressure. He grew suspicious of mere talk, which he found often led the therapy away from the key issues enacted in the body's movement. Jung, in his middle years, undergoing his own internal crisis, relied on the symbolic process, often building with stone or painting dream figures and other images from active imagination. Attention to the symbols, he found, bound and released energy.

Both believed that patients need to face their therapists and talk directly with them rather than employing Freud's couch method. In his early days treating the poor in Freud's clinic, Reich dealt with a working-class clientele for whom lying on a couch, with the analyst out of sight, was unworkable. Reich developed a direct, spontaneous, engaging style of therapeutic work that was useful in challenging resistance and stimulating the client's capacity for genuine contact. Jung also engaged the client directly, feeling that direct contact avoids an unnecessary transference. By facing the therapist, the client is able to more truly distinguish the therapist's genuine response from what is unconsciously assumed. Jung also believed that the therapist and client are "in the soup" together, and that both are changed in a successful therapy. Quite early, Jung acknowledged that countertransference cannot simply be sidestepped, but needs to be fully represented in the therapy.

Both painted pictures as a way of grasping their inner experiences more directly. Jung's paintings were an integral part of his own self-exploration. Reich, in his later years in Maine, painted to capture the images of energy he had come to see. In the 1930s in Scandinavia, he had been touched by the powerful work of Edvard Munch.

Both built houses to realize their visions externally. Reich built laboratories in Rangely, Maine, as the fulfillment of a dream for one who had wandered homeless from continent to continent. Rangely may have reminded Reich of the family farm he had lost in Austria years before and symbolically reconciled his scientific curiosity with his relatively untroubled early childhood. His home in Rangely gave Reich some sense of wholeness and protection, a retreat from the world.

Jung spent years developing his house in Bollingen, which represented a very powerful psychic symbol. Each change in the building signified a psychological and spiritual progression and provided an escape to a more primitive lifestyle.

Both were powerful prose writers. Both Jung and Reich wrote and published throughout extended professional careers. Jung, who had received an honorary doctorate from Harvard, was particularly pleased to receive a literature prize from Zurich.[12] Reich wrote in German until 1948. He was relieved to command sufficient fluency in English to be free of translators. He complained that his devoted translator, Theodore Wolfe, "smoothed out the 'climaxes' that Reich liked in writing."[13] Reich was disciplined in his writing habits, working a few hours every day except Sunday.[14]

Both were not only theoreticians but also gifted therapists and teachers. Both Reich and Jung were forceful, charismatic men, which was reflected in their teaching and therapy. By the age of twenty-five, Reich had established a technical seminar that brilliantly addressed essential issues of psychoanalytic work that previously had gone unexplored. Richard Sterba, once Reich's student and friend, recalls these seminars:

> At the same time that I began to see my first patient, in the fall of 1924, I started to attend the society meetings and the technical seminars that Wilhelm Reich had begun in 1922. Reich had the greatest influence on my development as a psychoanalytic therapist. He was an impressive personality full of youthful intensity. His clinical astuteness and technical skill made him an excellent teacher, and his technical seminar was so instructive that many of the older members of the society attended it regularly.[15]

Throughout his career, Reich continued to teach small groups of associates and do therapy. Myron Sharaf, Reich's biographer, recalls his therapy with Reich in the 1940s:

> I was extremely impressed by the way Reich worked with my body. He would have me breathe and then keep pointing out the way I avoided letting the breath expire naturally. Sometimes, he would press certain parts of my body, particularly my chest. A few times this was followed by very deep sobbing, crying in a way I could not remember ever having cried before. He would encourage me in an emphatic way. "Don't be ashamed of it. I have heard it by the millions. That sorrow is the best thing in you."[16]

Jung also taught associates in small seminars throughout his long career. Stories about him as a therapist abound. Joseph Henderson, a student, colleague, and friend of Jung's, remembers him as vigorous and ambitious in his early fifties, no longer so rigorously the scientist, but more the philosopher, a man rich in wisdom.[17] He was, writes Henderson, "a sort of humanist in the old Renaissance style, in whom an authentic scientist and artist met in a man of philosophic temperament and training. Above all, he was a humanist in action, not in theory."[18] Along with many others, Henderson was amazed at Jung's extraordinary power and intuition:

> There was, however, another aspect of Jung's character which refused to conform to European cultural patterns because it seemed to come totally from outside any culture. It seemed to burst upon him from an absolutely foreign but absolutely compelling primitive level of being. I think of it today (thanks to some of his own formulations) as the shaman which made Jung at times

into a man of uncanny perception and frightening unpredictability of behavior. This was the side which could never endure boredom and managed to keep him in hot water with someone all his life.[19]

Both had breakdowns following their breaks with Freud. By his own admission, Jung, following his break with Freud in 1913, entered into a long period of uncertainty, a confrontation with the unconscious that concluded around 1919. What he learned during those years became the basis of his later work and his autobiography, *Memories, Dreams, Reflections*, which describes this period in detail.[20]

Reich received a series of rebuffs from Freud in 1926. When he presented his manuscript of *The Function of the Orgasm* to Freud on the latter's seventieth birthday, on May 6th, Freud's only comment was "That thick?" Freud, who usually read manuscripts and returned them quickly, took several months to return Reich's. In the fall of 1926, Freud's book *Hemmung, Symptom und Angst* [Inhibitions, Symptoms, and Anxiety] was published, and in it Freud withdrew his earlier statements concerning stasis anxiety.[21] Since the unspoken procedure was always to build an idea on the structure of Freud's thought, Reich's somatic foothold had dramatically given way. "A relationship between actual anxiety and neurotic anxiety, Freud now said, could *not* be established."[22] In December 1926, in Freud's inner circle, Reich gave a presentation on character-analytic technique. Freud flatly contradicted him and insisted that rather than interpreting resistance first, one should interpret material as it appeared. This meeting was a crushing blow for Reich, and the conflict became even more severe early in 1927.

Many other factors are attributed to the conflict, including Reich's increasing interest in Marxist theory and social action. In addition, Reich, who was once a favorite son of Freud's, had requested personal analysis with him. While Freud had made a rule to no longer analyze those working with him, he had considered setting this rule aside, and it was crushing for Reich when Freud ultimately decided to stand by it. A further cause of conflict was the warring jealousies of other analysts, among them Dr. Paul Federn, who undermined Reich's favored position with Freud.

At this time, Reich developed tuberculosis of the lungs, a disease that killed his brother and father and represents the stress he felt. His physical breakdown allowed him to repair to a sanitorium in Davos, Switzerland, for a few months.

Both were interested in UFOs. As early as 1946, Jung had gathered information on UFOs. He was more interested in the fact that so many people were seeing round objects in the sky than in their physical existence. He considered the likelihood of mankind projecting the image of wholeness onto the sky as a way of healing the psychic injuries of our age:

> They [UFOs] are impressive manifestations of totality whose simple, round form portrays the archetype of the self, which we know from experience plays the chief role in uniting apparently irreconcilable opposites and is therefore best suited to compensate the split-mindedness of our age.[23]

Reich read a book on flying saucers in November 1953, Donald Keyhoe's *Flying Saucers from Outer Space*,[24] which confirmed what he had believed for some time: that life extended far beyond our planet. Myron Sharaf has written about this:

> He became convinced that the UFOs were "space ships" powered by orgone energy. He based this interpretation on certain observations that had been made of flying saucers: the bluish light shimmering through the openings of the machines, their comparatively silent motion, and the unusual maneuvers they were capable of making.[25]

Both wrote controversial books that were deeply thought out, but that were also personal outbursts not originally intended for publication. Reich wrote *Listen, Little Man!* in 1946. The book represented the enormous frustration he felt in dealing with small-mindedness and small-spiritedness from those suffering from emotional plague. While the book has some appeal, the tone is the most strident and self-revealing of all his writing, exposing his hurt and fatigue:

> When you hear about my orgone, you don't ask, "What can it do to cure the sick?" No, you ask, "Is he licensed to practice medicine in

the state of Maine?" Don't you realize that though you and your wretched licenses can obstruct my work a little, you can't stop it; that I have a worldwide reputation as the discoverer of your emotional plague and the investigator of your life energy; that no one is entitled to examine me unless he knows more than I do?[26]

Jung, in *The Answer to Job*, published in 1951, created a storm of reaction. He described Yahweh in his interaction with Job as morally inferior, less than human, only more powerful:

Truly, Yahweh can do all things and permits himself all things without batting an eyelid. With brazen countenance he can project his shadow side and remain unconscious at man's expense. . . . Murder and manslaughter are mere bagatelles, and if the mood takes him he can play the feudal grand seigneur and generously recompense his bondslave for the havoc wrought in his wheatfields. "So you have lost your sons and daughters? No harm done, I will give you new and better ones."[27]

Jung argued that Job was morally higher than God and so:

Yahweh must become man precisely because he has done man a wrong. He, the guardian of justice, knows that every wrong must be expiated, and Wisdom knows that moral law is above even him. Because his creature has surpassed him, he must regenerate himself.[28]

Both believed that work should determine one's say in the community. In the 1930s, Reich was living in Scandinavia, still with the Marxist sense of equality among workers and leadership. In his own organization, however, Reich was not about to relinquish his power, but argued that people had a voice in areas only where they contributed genuine work. Jung, as he grew older, found that the Jungian organization did not always represent his personal wishes. However, he refused to interfere in areas where he was not contributing to the actual work. In that way, he avoided undermining the authority that had developed from hard work. In developing the C. G. Jung Institute in 1948, Jung drew up the statutes that established an executive body, called the curatorium, that ran the institute. This concentration of power in the hands of the curatorium was opposed by many of Jung's followers, but Jung remained firm on the point, for he saw, writes his biographer and close friend Barbara Hannah, that "the *people who did the work must have the power*, that anything else would lead to abuse of power, which was the great danger he feared in allowing his psychology to be given a worldly form like the institute."[29]

Both were interested in the electrical charge of the skin and in the effect of emotions on the charge. While Jung was at Burghölzli Hospital in 1904, he began to use Wundt's word association test in a novel way. To establish the presence of complexes and so establish the reality of the unconscious, patients were asked to give associations to words. Their responses were timed, and significant deviations from the average time were keys to unconscious interference. In a further level of sophistication, he used equipment to measure the electrical charge of the skin, and deviation in skin charge was found to correlate significantly with time deviations. Because of his work with association, Jung was asked to lecture in the United States and was able to travel with Freud in 1909 to Clark University, where they both lectured.

Reich had wanted to establish the bioelectrical nature of the sexual response and study sexual pleasure. In the laboratory of the Psychological Institute at the University of Oslo in 1935, Reich carried out experiments utilizing the psychogalvanic phenomenon. He was able to establish that in an erogenous zone of the body, mere tumescence does not increase the electrical potential. Only when the subjective response of sexual excitement and pleasure was present did the electrical potential increase. Reich was able to measure what had before been subjective responses (pleasure and anxiety) and show that there is a bioelectrical charge to the movement of libido in the body.

Both took pride in being in the military. Reich, of course, lost his Austrian farm during the First World War and was recruited into the army as an adolescent. The experience was a positive one despite the personal losses. Ilse Ollendorff Reich, his third wife, has written about this:

> I think, on the whole, he enjoyed his military life. He was not a pacifist by nature, and the responsibility for a group of people was

much to his liking. He saw active duty on the Italian front, and sometimes told how they were shelled for days at a time. . . . He remembered the very cooperative Italian girls. . . . He must have liked wearing an officer's uniform. He told us that even though he was in the infantry, he always wore spurs. . . . I have a feeling that at that time his social conscience was not very developed, and that he took the war in stride without bothering much about the rights and wrongs.[30]

Jung, as a Swiss citizen, participated for years in guarding the country. Barbara Hannah remarks on it in her biography:

Throughout the war, Jung repeatedly had periods of military service, which he performed with great enthusiasm. To him one of the drawbacks of getting old was that he was over the age for military service in World War II, although he was still quite well and active enough until his severe illness in 1944.[31]

Both came from parents who were unhappy in their marriage, and both had one other sibling. Jung's sister Gertrud was born when Jung was nine. His early years were as an only child. Jung's parents slept in separate rooms, and Jung shared a room with his father. When his father died in 1896, Jung took it upon himself not only to continue his schooling but to support his mother and twelve-year-old sister. "My parents' marriage," he wrote, "was not a happy one, but full of trials and difficulties and tests of patience. Both made the mistakes typical of many couples."[32] Jung's father had studied Oriental languages in Göttingen and completed a dissertation, in Arabic, on the "Song of Songs." His happiness appears to have ended with his student days. His marriage was a great disappointment. Both Jung's parents worked hard at being devout, "with the result," wrote their son, "that there were angry scenes between them only too frequently."[33]

Reich was three years older than his brother Robert. They appear to have had a competitive but friendly relationship. The father was a fascinating, vital, dominating man, given to rages. His abuse and jealousy unfortunately predominated in this unhappy marriage.[34] Both Reich's and Jung's siblings died early: Robert at 26; Gertrud at 41.

Both had eczema as children. Reich's incurable eczema lasted his entire life and was perhaps related to the marital tension in his childhood home. His father, a jealous, tyrannical man, often flew into rages that intimidated his wife. Reich's mother's suicide may have established the eczema permanently.

In *Memories, Dreams, Reflections*, Jung recalled a childhood period of eczema following the temporary loss of his mother, who was hospitalized when he was three years old. He was also painfully aware of the unhappiness of his parents' marriage:

> I was suffering, so my mother told me afterward, from general eczema. Dim intimations of trouble in my parents' marriage hovered around me. My illness, in 1878, must have been connected with a temporary separation from my parents.[35]

Both suffered from tachycardia. Reich suffered from it in the late 1940s. He smoked incessantly until his heart attack in 1951, when he finally quit for good. Ilse Ollendorff Reich reports an attack in 1949:

> In February he had several severe attacks of tachycardia, and several blackouts from coughing paroxysms. He decided to cut down on his excessive smoking, but did not succeed too well with his resolve. He did not feel that his physical symptoms were the result of overwork. He thought, rather, that they were due to a fear that his efforts would be lost through misuse, misinterpretation, or degeneration.[36]

Jung also suffered from tachycardia in his later years. In February 1944, he slipped in the snow and was hospitalized with a broken fibula. Eleven days later, he suffered from a bad thrombosis of the heart and several others that went to the lungs. In November 1946, he suffered a second heart attack, which was followed by attacks of tachycardia. Barbara Hannah has written of this period:

> After his illness, he told me that he was doubtful if he had really had a heart infarct. At all events, it was mainly a disturbance of the vegetative nervous system that had the effect of giving him attacks of tachycardia (racing of the pulse). He again found himself con-

fronted, like medicine men all over the world, with curing himself. The doctors insisted that it was another heart infarct; and he was thus forced to find out for himself what was really the matter and how it should be met. Once again he said that he had an illness because he was faced with the mysterious problem of the *hieros gamos* (the *mysterium coniunctionis*).[37]

Both erupted unexpectedly into rages in their later years. Reich is reported by Ilse Ollendorff to have exploded unexpectedly in jealous rages during their marriage. When he was under attack by the Scandinavian press in the late 1930s, he apparently took out his frustration on Elsa Lindenberg, his second wife. Later, in the late 1940s and early 1950s, under attack in America, he exploded at Ilse. Eventually, he began drinking heavily at night, angrily accusing her of infidelity, a combination that drove her away in 1953.

Jung also occasionally exploded in rage in his old age, asking the indulgence of his housekeeper for what he realized were peculiar uncontrolled eruptions. Vincent Brome has written of this:

> At the outset, Jung said to Miss Bailey: "Now, there's one thing you must understand. I am a man who can get into great rages. Take no notice of them. They don't mean anything. And I soon get out of them." His "terrible temper" quickly became evident.[38]

Notes

1. C. P. Snow, *The Two Cultures; and A Second Look* (Cambridge, England: Cambridge University Press, 1969), p. 7.

2. C. G. Jung, *The Structure and Dynamics of the Psyche*, 2nd ed., trans. R. F. C. Hull, Bollingen Series XX, vol. 8 (Princeton: Princeton University Press, 1969), p. 509.

3. Wilhelm Reich, *The Function of the Orgasm*, trans. Theodore P. Wolfe (New York: Meridian, 1970), p. 51.

4. C. G. Jung, "Letter to Henry A. Murray, September 10, 1935," in *C. G. Jung Letters*, vol. 1 (1906–1950), trans. R. F. C. Hull, ed. Gerhard Adler and Aniela Jaffé, Bollingen Series XCV (Princeton: Princeton University Press, 1973), p. 200.

5. Wilhelm Reich, *Cosmic Superimposition*, trans. Mary Boyd Higgins and Therese Pol (New York: Farrar, Straus & Giroux, 1973), p. 280.

6. C. G. Jung, *The Archetypes and the Collective Unconscious*, trans. R. F. C. Hull, ed. Sir Herbert Read, Michael Fordham, and Gerhard Adler, Bollingen Series XX, vol. 9 (Princeton: Princeton University Press, 1980), pp. 95–96.

7. Wilhelm Reich, *Ether, God, and Devil*, trans. Mary Boyd Higgins and Therese Pol (New York: Farrar, Straus & Giroux, 1973), pp. 137–138 (italics in the original).

8. Wilhelm Reich, *The Mass Psychology of Fascism*, trans. Vincent R. Carfagno (New York: Farrar, Straus & Giroux, 1970), p. 111.

9. Wilhelm Reich, *Character Analysis*, 3rd ed., trans. Theodore P. Wolfe (New York: Farrar, Straus & Giroux, 1949), p. 251.

10. Reich, *Ether, God, and Devil*, p. 4.

11. Jung, *Structure and Dynamics*, p. 216.

12. See Barbara Hannah, *Jung: His Life and Work—A Biographical Memoir* (New York: Putnam's, 1976), p. 207: "In 1932 the city of Zurich awarded Jung its literature prize. This pleased him far more than much more famous honors, such as the honorary doctorates which were increasingly bestowed on him from abroad, because it was the first recognition from his own country."

13. Myron Sharaf, *Fury on Earth: A Biography of Wilhelm Reich* (New York: St. Martin's Press, 1983), p. 267.

14. Ibid.

15. Richard F. Sterba, *Reminiscences of a Viennese Psychoanalyst* (Detroit: Wayne State University Press, 1982), p. 34.

16. Sharaf, *Fury on Earth*, p. 24.

17. Joseph L. Henderson, "C. G. Jung: A Personal Evaluation," in *Contact with Jung*, ed. Michael Fordham (Philadelphia: Lippincott, 1963), p. 222.

18. Ibid., p. 221.

19. Ibid., p. 222.

20. C. G. Jung, *Memories, Dreams, Reflections*, revised edition, trans. Richard and Clara Winston, ed. Aniela Jaffé (New York: Pantheon, 1973).

21. See Sigmund Freud, *The Problem of Anxiety*, trans. Henry Alden Bunker, M.D. (New York: W. W. Norton, 1936).

22. Reich, *Function of the Orgasm*, p. 112.

23. C. G. Jung, *Flying Saucers: A Myth of Things Seen in the Skies*, trans. R. F. C. Hull, Bollingen Series XX, vol. 10 (Princeton: Princeton University Press, 1978), p. 21.

24. Donald Keyhoe, *Flying Saucers from Outer Space* (New York: Henry Holt, 1953).

25. Sharaf, *Fury on Earth*, p. 413.

26. Wilhelm Reich, *Listen, Little Man!* trans. Ralph Manheim (New York: Farrar, Straus & Giroux, 1974), p. 53.

27. C. G. Jung, *The Answer to Job*, trans. R. F. C. Hull, Bollingen Series XX, vol. 11 (Princeton: Princeton University Press, 1973), p. 20.

28. Ibid., p. 40.

29. Hannah, *Jung*, p. 298 (italics in the original).

30. Ilse Ollendorff Reich, *Wilhelm Reich: A Personal Biography* (New York: St. Martin's Press, 1969), p. 5.

31. Hannah, *Jung*, p. 126.

32. Jung, *Memories, Dreams, Reflections*, p. 315.

33. Ibid., p. 91.

34. Sharaf, *Fury on Earth*, p. 37.

35. Jung, *Memories, Dreams, Reflections*, p. 8.

36. Ilse Ollendorff Reich, *Wilhelm Reich*, p. 93.

37. Hannah, *Jung*, p. 294.

38. Vincent Brome, *Jung: Man and Myth* (New York: Atheneum, 1978), p. 262.

Chapter 3

Genitality

God will not have his work made manifest by cowards.

—Ralph Waldo Emerson, "Self-Reliance"

Unfortunately, in the unfolding drama of Western culture, the mind of man has become divorced from his body. Sexuality, in particular, has been linked with an undesirable animal element, a demonic force that corrupts man's true spiritual nature. But just as Western culture has denied the value of sexuality, psychoanalysis has denied the value of spirituality. Freud and Reich, impressed with the force of the sexual instinct, rejected spiritual realities as an illusion culturally induced through sexual repression.

Jung, on the other hand, saw sexuality and spirituality as a polarity in man's psyche. Denied or accepted, in man's psyche there are images of the gods. Whether God exists outside the psyche of man was an issue that Jung preferred to leave to the theologians, but he included sexuality in his pantheon as a dark chthonic god. When he was a child, he dreamed of descending an old stone staircase in a field, finally standing at the foot of a huge one-eyed fleshy form, an ithyphallus. Jung's awareness of spiritual realities was thrust upon him through painful, confusing visions and dreams. Like Reich, Jung lived out his sexual nature. Both men were noted for their healthy, earthy constitutions.

Central to Reich's thought throughout his entire multifaceted career were his views on sexuality. From the early 1920s, he saw libido as a biological, measurable energy, not merely a useful abstraction. In the 1930s, he was able to measure it as a bioelectrical energy. And by the 1940s, he had extended sexual energy to encompass the invisible ether of the universe: orgone energy. Life in its abundance was suspended, he believed, in an invisible orgone ocean. The genital embrace—that is, sexual intercourse—which fascinated Reich at the beginning of his career in the 1920s, still commanded a chapter in *The Murder of Christ*, written in the 1950s, toward the end of his life.[1]

Reich's attention to sexuality and the genital embrace was encouraged neither by the culture nor by his psychoanalytic comrades. To many, his focus appeared too narrow, his approach too belligerent. He believed that all neurosis was caused by an unholy alliance between a psychic conflict and dammed-up sexual energy, that the blocking of the life force in the very tissue of the body was the cause of the misery in the psyche of man and his world. His undeviating concern for sexuality can be better understood by considering his early life.

Reich was raised with his younger brother Robert on a farm in the Ukrainian part of Austria. They were apparently somewhat isolated from children their age. Like many other Jewish families of the late nineteenth century in the Austrian Empire, the Reichs had become "assimilated" into the German culture of the day, stepping away from their own religious tradition. Since the father aspired to greater social heights, the sons were dissuaded from playing either with peasants or with Jews, and they were provided with private tutors.

As a child, Reich was very attached to his mother, who has been described as attractive but weak. His father, on the other hand, has been portrayed as a rigid, tense, and violent man of considerable competence and intelligence.[2]

In early adolescence, through his own unwitting sexual curiosity, Reich precipitated some brutal events that unconsciously dominated him for many years. He discovered that his mother was having an affair with his tutor. Myron Sharaf, in his biography of Reich, has accurately deduced the tragic story of Reich's involvement in his parents' deaths, as described in *Passion of Youth*, Reich's recently published autobiography of his early years.[3] Sharaf also draws our attention to a thinly disguised autobiographical account that Reich presented as a paper to his medical school seminar on sexuality, published in 1920, called "A Case of Pubertal Breaching of the Incest Taboo." In this veiled form, we gain a glimpse into his childhood home:

> He was raised very strictly by his father, always having to achieve more than his siblings in order to satisfy his father's ambition to have industrious children. From earliest childhood, a deep tenderness bound him to his mother, and it was she who often protected him from the violent excesses of his father. His parents' marriage was not a happy one: his mother "suffered terribly" because of his father's jealousy.[4]

As the mother's affair progressed, according to the account, the boy was tormented by the terrible secret. "Either it was my unconscious hate of Father or the erotic tingling involved in being party to such a horrible secret that prevented my telling Father anything."[5] When the father went away for three weeks, the boy spied on the lovers:

> I heard his door open, and close partially. Then all was quiet. I jumped out of bed and crept after her, freezing, with my teeth chattering from cold and fear and horror. Slowly I made my way to the door of his room. It was ajar. I stood there and listened. . . . I heard them kissing, whispering, and the horrible creaking of the bed in which my mother lay. . . .
>
> All I remember of that catastrophic night is that I wanted to rush into the room, but was held back by the thought: They might kill you! I recall having read that a lover will kill anyone who disturbs him. With a head full of bizarre fantasies, I crept back to bed without hope of consolation, my youthful spirit broken.
>
> And so it happened, night after night. I followed her to his door and waited there until morning. Gradually I became accustomed to it (!!). My horror gave place to erotic feelings. Once I even considered breaking in on them and demanding that she have intercourse with me too (shame!), threatening that otherwise I would tell Father.[6]

Reich, the youth, brutally questioned by his suspicious father, confessed his mother's infidelity. From January to October of 1910, his mother endured terrible physical and verbal abuse. "During that period," Reich later wrote, "her face, hands, and body bore the marks of [my father's] rage."[7] She finally committed suicide by taking poison, and his heartbroken father died a few years later of tubercular complications following financial setbacks.

Elsa Lindenberg, in an interview with Myron Sharaf in 1962, indicated that "even into his thirties, Reich would sometimes wake in the night overwhelmed by the thought that he had 'killed' his mother."[8]

Sharaf recorded another significant event from an interview with Reich's brother's wife, Ottilie. As a soldier stationed in an Italian town, Reich for the first time experienced a full, loving, sexual embrace, which he later described as "orgastic potency."

> Reich recalled to Ottilie the experience of a sexual embrace with a young woman in the Italian village where he was stationed in 1916. Reich went on to comment that he had been having sexual intercourse for some years before this relationship and that he had enjoyed it, but that this woman was different from any he had known before. For the first time, he experienced the full meaning of love. Also for the first time, he was to experience what he would later name and describe in detail—and for which he was to fight so hard—"orgastic potency." But in 1916 he found the experience very hard to put into words.[9]

Richard Sterba, Reich's student and friend during the 1920s, has suggested another reason why Reich may have been intent on the orgasm theory:

> I think Reich drew the thesis of mental hygienic influence out of his own experience. He told me once that if he did not have an orgasm for two days, he felt physically unwell and "saw black before his eyes" like before an approaching spell of fainting. These symptoms disappeared immediately with an orgasmic experience.[10]

After his father's death, Reich was able to run the farm until war came; but he lost it when Austria was defeated. As a medical student in Vienna after the war, often without money for food, and wearing his army uniform as civilian clothing, Reich was granted the privilege, as a soldier, to complete the six-year medical program in four years.

In January 1919, Reich and some other medical students formed a sexological seminar in order to counteract the neglect of the subject in the medical school curriculum. By that summer, Reich had delivered a paper on "Concepts of Libido from Forel to Jung," and was made the seminar leader. In his meetings with sexologists, Reich was enormously struck by Freud, who "spoke to me like an ordinary human being. He had piercingly intelligent eyes; they did not try to penetrate the listener's eyes in a visionary pose; they simply looked into the world, straight and honest."[11]

In 1920, Reich was granted membership in the Psychoanalytic Society, a considerable honor for a young man who was only twenty-three, still a medical student, and impoverished, among colleagues twenty years his senior. He directed his attention in a literal and concrete way to the study of sexuality. It is not exactly clear how Reich, amid such rich and speculative minds, could have held to a rigid, biological reductionism, or why he should have developed so intense a focus on sexual specifics. He described himself as a mechanist in his medical studies and "in my thinking rather too systematic. In the preclinical subjects, I was most interested in systematic and topographic anatomy. . . . At the same time, however, I was fascinated by metaphysics."[12] He also commented that he annoyed some of his colleagues by "desultoriness" and "illogicality of thought."[13]

As a psychoanalytic student, Reich was assigned patients from the working class, who were unable to pay very much for service. By 1922, he worked in a newly established psychoanalytic clinic, which borrowed its rooms from a heart clinic in order to provide analysis to those who could not otherwise afford it. In those antiseptic medical rooms, dealing with the impoverished working class, Reich was involved in a different psychology than the older, more experienced members of the profession, who, in the comforts of their studies, had begun to deal with the rich and famous.

The pragmatic focus on sexual malfunction was more suited to the austerity of the medical office. In addition, Reich was constantly exposed to the sociological hardship and pain of his clients, whereas Freud and the older, "distinguished" members were consistently insulated from the crueler aspects of Viennese life. Thus, Reich was more likely than his colleagues to be awakened to sociological concerns, both as a poor young student seeking a place for himself in the world and as a doctor exposed day after day to the pain and impoverishment of Vienna. It is no wonder that in later years he said he was a "shark in a pond of carps."[14]

The pressure of his initial poverty, his youth, his appalling thrust from puberty to adulthood through the suicide of his mother and indirect suicide of his father, his student status working with the poor, and his aggressive predisposition toward concreteness of mind did not leave him well-disposed toward the more worldly, benign, abstract, indirect, diplomatic Viennese mind. But in whatever way we try to explain Reich's single-minded focus on sexuality, it appears to unfold inevitably out of the very nature of his developing thought and is not finally accountable to any external event. Reich himself said:

> I became convinced that the enduring, indestructible core of psychoanalysis is its sexual theory, just because it was and still is the issue of the doctrine most fiercely attacked. Coming to Freud from sexology and biology, I perhaps felt the lack of a fundamental theory of the biological basis of neurosis more acutely than did my colleagues who came from internal medicine or from materialistic philosophy.[15]

Reich supported Freud's conclusion that the central psychic conflict was the sexual child-parent relationship,[16] but his experience had taught him that working through the psychic conflict was not enough.

For example, Reich told of working with a waiter who suffered from a complete lack of erection. In the third year of therapy, the "primal scene" was reconstructed. Reich's work was commended by his older colleagues, and yet the waiter remained impotent and was discharged uncured.[17] However, a fortuitous event had happened with another patient that caught Reich's attention. He had analyzed a young student whose compulsive "rumination immediately turned into compulsive associating. It looked pretty hopeless. After some time, an incest phantasm broke through, and for the first time the patient masturbated with satisfaction. With that, all the symptoms disappeared suddenly."[18]

Reich gradually developed a theory that the pathology of a psychic conflict depends upon whether there is a full and adequate sexual discharge. Psychic conflict alone does not create neurosis, he argued. Neurosis depends on dammed-up sexual energy to provide the necessary biological energy. With a simple river analogy,

Reich illustrated the dramatic role that sexual energy plays in neurosis:

> The strength, shape, and breadth of a river system are determined chiefly by their sources. If the springs are plentiful, and lie high in the mountains, and if, perhaps, there are glaciers, the stream will develop a stronger flow, a swifter current, and will build up more energy than if the sources are meager and located in flat land. What is important about a river, in terms of natural science, is not whether it can take barges or only small boats, nor whether it winds five times or ten, nor whether it divides at its mouth into two or into eight branches, nor whether it is ten miles long or a hundred. All these characteristics depend fundamentally on only two factors: the abundance and strength of the springs and the shape of the terrain through which the streams must make their way. If the amount of water flowing off through the river system always corresponds to the amount issuing from the springs, then the energy of the fall will always equalize. No more flows in than can flow out.[19]

Reich argued that, to some degree, the outflow can be regulated and exploited without danger. However, if the water is seriously obstructed from its natural outflow, then what emerges is "uncontrollable, unnatural, and destructive forces."[20]

Reich could not understand why Freud would pull away from the concrete biological model of sexuality in favor of theoretical formulations. Freud had once assumed the existence of chemical sexual substances "which not correctly metabolized caused physical irregularities such as anxiety and heart palpitations."[21] Reich, who was concerned with establishing the sexual etiology of all neurosis, was frustrated by each new Freudian formulation:

> In 1923, Freud's *The Ego and the Id* was published. Its immediate effect on practice, which constantly had to deal with the patients' sexual difficulties, was confusing. In practice, one did not know what to do with the "superego" or "unconscious guilt feelings"; they were theoretical formulations concerning very obscure facts. There was no technical procedure for dealing with these. One preferred to deal with fear of masturbation or sexual guilt feelings.[22]

Reich was also deeply concerned that psychology establish itself as a natural science. He was painfully aware that "leading psychopathologists, like Jaspers, contended that psychological interpretation of meaning, and thus psychoanalysis, were not within the realm of natural science at all."[23] Reich argued that natural science "dealt only with *quantities* and energies, philosophy with psychic *qualities*; and there was no bridge between."[24] From Reich's perspective, Freud disdained to enter into such philosophical discussions, while Reich argued against "the enemy" who classified the psychoanalysts as just another philosophical school. "But," says Reich, "we knew that—for the first time in the history of psychology—we were engaging in natural science. We wanted to be taken seriously."[25] Reich sought a biological basis for libido and the issue of anxiety. In November 1923, he delivered a paper on "genitality" in which he asserted that the genital disturbance was the most important symptom of neurosis. While he was talking, he became increasingly aware of a "chilling of the atmosphere" at the meeting:

> My assertion that the genital disturbance was an important and perhaps the most important symptom of the neurosis was erroneous, they said. Even worse, they said, was my contention that an evaluation of genitality provided prognostic and therapeutic criteria. Two analysts bluntly asserted that they knew any number of female patients with a completely healthy sex life![26]

Between 1922 and 1926, Reich consolidated his orgasm theory piece-by-piece as he sought a concrete formulation of Freud's concept of psychic energy. Challenged publicly, Reich was driven to establish the criteria for a true orgastic potency:

> Erective and ejaculative potency are nothing but indispensable prerequisites for *orgastic potency*. Orgastic potency is the *capacity for surrender to the flow of biological energy without any inhibition*, the capacity for *complete discharge of all dammed-up sexual excitation* through *involuntary pleasurable contractions of the body*. Not a single neurotic individual possesses orgastic potency; the corollary of this fact is the fact that the vast majority of humans suffer from a character-neurosis.[27]

In 1924, at the Psychoanalytic Congress in Salzburg, Reich introduced his concept of orgastic potency, which he said was well received.[28] He saw neurosis as a disturbance not only in sexuality in general but specifically in genital function. Sterba recalls the paper, which, "presented in a forceful manner, left me with an impression more of the power of the speaker than of the content."[29] Although Sterba was not terribly impressed by Reich's concept of genitality, he was intoxicated at the conference by the atmosphere of greatness: "The atmosphere of the congress made me feel that I was witness to and participant in a cause that would be of tremendous consequence for the whole of mankind once it was generally recognized and became influential in all fields of human study."[30]

Around 1925, Reich saw a cleavage in the Society. After Freud's *The Ego and the Id*, a demoralizing shift had begun. Clinical discussions were few. Outsiders spoke "who had never done an analysis and gave high-sounding talks on the ego and superego, or on schizophrenia they had never seen. Sexuality became an empty shell, the concept of 'libido' became devoid of any sexual content and turned into an empty phrase."[31] Reich noticed even more personal intrigue and behind-the-scenes political tactics. Unfortunately, he did not notice the powerful changes Freud was going through. Freud had undergone the first in a series of painful cancer operations a few years earlier and was suffering from a poor-fitting oral prosthesis that inhibited his speaking. Reich was seemingly unaware of Freud's fear concerning his own death, and was also unaware of Freud's suffering from the loss of Rank, his closest working companion. That loss was, in part, responsible for the political intrigue as members jockeyed about in an attempt to replace Rank. Reich, who had access to Freud on a private basis, admired Freud and remained grateful to him, but does not seem to have considered Freud's perspective as an old man in pain.

Sterba's view of that period is entirely different from Reich's. In January 1925, the training institute of the Vienna Psychoanalytic Society opened under the direction of Helene Deutsch. "The program of lectures and seminars presented by the Institute," writes Sterba, "was very rich and was given by the best minds in the field in Vienna."[32] Siegfried Bernfeld, Herman Nunberg, Paul Federn, Theodor Reik, Robert Waelder, and Eduard Hitschmann gave lectures, and Sterba was utterly enchanted. However, he reported that Reich's training seminars were the most valuable: "The most instructive part of the curriculum for me remained the bi-weekly seminar of continuous case presentations conducted by Wilhelm Reich."[33]

At the same time, Freud was being courted by the rich and famous, receiving offers that, at the very least, must have been unsettling for him. Celia Bertin, in her biography of Marie Bonaparte, comments on these offers:

> Freud was now so famous that Hollywood asked him to cooperate in writing scripts based on world-famous love stories, starting with Anthony and Cleopatra. He also received proposals ("an incalculable number of dollars," his daughter Mathilde later told Marie Bonaparte) from Hearst and the *Chicago Tribune* to follow the trial of Leopold and Loeb and give a diagnosis of them. In the following year, the Danish literary critic George Brandes made the trip to Vienna to see him, and Freud met the Indian philosopher-poet Rabindranath Tagore.[34]

Freud was not responsive to Reich's manuscript of *The Function of the Orgasm*, presented to him on his seventieth birthday, May 6, 1926. Reich was devastated when he did not receive Freud's full endorsement. "One can notice an increased coolness," he wrote. "At first I did not understand. Why should Freud reject the 'orgasm theory,' which was enthusiastically welcomed by most of the younger analysts?"[35] Sterba does not concur with Reich that the younger analysts enthusiastically endorsed the "orgasm theory":

> Another unacceptable theory of Wilhelm Reich's which he pursued with increasing fanaticism was his conviction that a perfect orgasm will prevent or cure any form of neurosis. Freud himself pointed out to Reich, in one of the meetings at the Berggasse 19, the fact that many neurotogenic drives, particularly pregenital ones, cannot be discharged, even by the most perfect orgasm. The general observation that some neurotics, particularly compulsives, can have impeccable orgasms without being cured by them did not make any inroad on Reich's conviction concerning the healing and preventive function of orgasm. Mockingly we younger analysts spoke of Reich's "genital paradise." In my opinion, he defended his thesis so rigorously because his character corresponded very much to the "genital narcissist," which he so well described in one of his papers.[36]

Reich's "genital paradise" took a sociological form when he came upon the writings of Bronislaw Malinowski on the nature versus nurture controversy. Reich was strongly for nurture. "*The basis of the puberty problem is sociological, not biological,"* he wrote. "Nor does it lie in the child-parent conflict, as is assumed by psychoanalysis."[37] From Malinowski's *The Sexual Life of Savages* (1929), Reich found "a wealth of material which confronted the world with the fact that sexual repression is sociological and not of biological origin."[38] Reich's naive optimism is blatantly apparent in his description of the Trobriand natives. He saw in the Trobriand Islands an entire society of healthy genital characters, because the problem of sex repression was resolved, and—as Malinowski maintained as well—the Oedipal complex was absent because of sociological structure. What was evil in man was exogenic, induced by cultural repression:

> Children in the Trobriand Islands know no sex repression and no sexual secrecy. Their sex life is allowed to develop naturally, freely, and unhampered *through every stage of life, with full satisfaction.* The children engage freely in the sexual activities which correspond to their age. Nonetheless, or rather just for this reason, the society of the Trobrianders knew, in the third decade of our century, no sexual perversions, no functional psychoses, no psychoneuroses, no sex murder; they have no word for theft; homosexuality and masturbation, to them, mean nothing but an unnatural and imperfect means of sexual gratification, a sign of a disturbed capacity to reach normal satisfaction. To the children of the Trobrianders, the strict, obsessional training for excremental control which undermines the civilization of the white race is unknown. The Trobrianders, therefore, are *spontaneously* clean, orderly, social without compulsion, intelligent, and industrious. The socially accepted form of sexual life is spontaneous monogamy without compulsion, a relationship which can be dissolved without difficulties; thus, there is no promiscuity.[39]

Some of the same optimism has been noted by Derek Freeman in *Margaret Mead and Samoa*, which lays bare the historical underpinnings promoting the extreme distortions that flourished in the late 1920s.[40] Freeman maintains that Mead's view of Samoa idealized and distorted the true nature of the people.

City dwellers, of course, for centuries have idealized the pastoral life. In sixteenth-century England, aristocrats attempted to return to the "gentle innocence" of nature by dressing up as shepherds and shepherdesses in extended parties. The unconscious easily projects out on whatever it does not understand and creates its own reality.

It was easy to dismiss Reich's attention to genital functioning as a naive oversimplification, easy to discount his work, as Sterba and Freud and the psychoanalysts did, and, to their own detriment, to overlook the sexual, physiological component in neurosis, for which they had no adequate, effective response. While Freud rejected Reich's genital formula, his own technique failed to resolve a genital conflict with one of his most devoted and intimate followers, Marie Bonaparte.

Marie Bonaparte was married to Prince George of Greece, who was homosexually inclined, with no sexual interest in the princess. She was an attractive woman, who resolved this misfortune through discreet affairs. Nevertheless, she was aggravated by frigidity. She investigated the work of Professor Halban of Vienna, a biologist and surgeon, and in 1924 wrote an article under a pseudonym promoting his solution to frigidity.[41] She described how, although some frigidity could be cured by psychotherapy, in some cases the clitoris is too great a distance from the opening of the vagina, and surgery is required to move the clitoris nearer to the urethral passage. In 1925, "The Princess," as she became known in the Freudian circle, managed, through connections in Paris with psychoanalysts there, to arrange to be seen by Freud. She was described by Dr. René Laforgue, a psychoanalyst who had frequent "chats" with her, as having an obsessional neurosis. She received Laforgue confined to her bed after a series of operations: the removal of an ovarian cyst, some plastic surgery to "correct" her breasts, and the retouching of a scar at the base of her nose. Laforgue also felt that she had "a marked virility complex."[42]

At the end of September 1925, Marie Bonaparte began therapy with Freud. They had immediate rapport, and he soon acceded to her request to meet with him two hours a day. He told her that she was bisexual, which helped her to understand men, "having a man in herself."[43]

> "The analysis is the most 'gripping' thing I have ever done. Ich bin, as they say in German, gepackt! aber vollstandig," she wrote to Laforgue in October 1925, but she gave him no details. Before the end of October, she handed over to Freud the five copybooks from

her childhood, for him to decipher and reconstruct their lost meaning. Once she had come to know the nature of her unconscious conflicts, she would be freed to act, and to learn a profession that would allow her to realize her potentialities. She also hoped to be cured of her failures in love. She had come to her teacher in search of "the penis and orgastic normality."[44]

In the third week, after she presented a dream, Freud told her "that she had witnessed adults in the act of intercourse as a young child. She objected violently, but Freud assured her that several of her associations were confirmatory as the analysis proceeded."[45] Her copybooks confirmed for Freud that Marie had witnessed the primal scene, and that the protagonists were the groom Pascal and her nursemaid. After further therapy, she returned to Paris and confronted Pascal, who under pressure confirmed all of Freud's deductions. But even with the primal scene reconstructed and its implications analyzed, the Princess apparently found her frigidity still unthawed.

In the early months of 1927, she let Professor Halban surgically move her clitoris closer to her vagina. Freud was not at all pleased. The operation marked the "end of the honeymoon with analysis."[46] While their deep friendship bridged the gap, her sexual functioning was not improved either by analysis or by surgery. By 1929, there was still no improvement:

> She observed at this time that "work is easy and sexual pleasure difficult." "Psychoanalysis can at the most bring resignation, and I am forty-six years old," she wrote in one of her notebooks. "The analysis has brought me peace of mind, of heart, and the possibility of working, but from the physiological point of view nothing. I am thinking of a second operation. Must I give up sex? Work, write, analyze? But absolute chastity frightens me."[47]

In the 1930s, Freud said to a student: "My discoveries are not primarily a heal-all. My discoveries are a basis for a very grave philosophy. There are very few who understand this, *there are very few who are capable of understanding this*."[48]

Reich was young. He had not become resigned to failure. We can, of course, speculate what results would have occurred had the Princess transferred her analysis to him. She had met Reich, excited by the opportunity, at a meeting in 1926 where he made a presentation before Freud and a chosen few. But Reich, while a good educator around sexuality in the 1920s, worked vigorously with resistance and character analysis. He had considerable success with clients suffering from sexual dysfunction, but only in the 1930s did he develop body techniques that released the physiological embeddedness of neurosis—techniques he called vegetotherapy.

In 1933 in Scandinavia, having separated from his first wife and his two children, having left Germany because of Hitler's victories, at war with the Psychoanalytic Institute, at war with his ex-wife Annie, at war with the Nazis, and at war with the Communist leadership both in Germany and Scandinavia,[49] Reich fortunately found some refuge as a teacher of his character-analytic method. He had grown more physical and more relaxed around touching the body and requesting physical expression. He identified working with a patient in Copenhagen in 1933 as the moment of breakthrough:

> In Copenhagen, 1933, I treated a man who put up especially strong resistances against the uncovering of his passive-homosexual phantasies. This resistance was manifested in an extreme attitude of stiffness of the neck ("stiff-necked"). After an energetic attack upon his resistance, he suddenly gave in, but in a rather alarming manner. For three days, he presented severe manifestations of vegetative shock. The color of his face kept changing rapidly from white to yellow or blue; the skin was mottled and of various tints; he had severe pains in the neck and the occiput; the heartbeat was rapid; he had diarrhea, felt worn out, and seemed to have lost hold. I was disturbed. . . . Affects had broken through somatically after the patient had yielded in a psychic defense attitude. The stiff neck, expressing an attitude of tense masculinity, apparently had bound vegetative energies which now broke loose in an uncontrolled and disordered fashion.[50]

From this experience and others, Reich came to see that muscular hypertension and character attitudes serve the same function psychically; they were functionally identical and could not be separated.

From now on, I was able to make practical use of this unity. When a character inhibition would fail to respond to psychic influencing, I would work at the corresponding somatic attitude. Conversely, when a disturbing muscular attitude proved difficult of access, I would work on its characterological expression and thus loosen it up.[51]

In vegetotherapy, Reich watched the flow of energy in the body. He worked with the breathing pattern to release chronic contraction in the tissue, which arrests the pulsation found naturally in life. Breathing, like the heartbeat, establishes the body's rhythm and flow. The natural uninterrupted streaming of the body's energy Reich called the orgasm reflex, which became the biological goal of vegetotherapy and the basis for dissolving neurotic conflict.

Notes

1. Wilhelm Reich, *The Murder of Christ* [vol. 1 of *The Emotional Plague of Mankind*] (New York: Simon & Schuster, 1953).

2. See Myron Sharaf, *Fury on Earth: A Biography of Wilhelm Reich* (New York: St. Martin's Press, 1983); and Ilse Ollendorff Reich, *Wilhelm Reich: A Personal Biography* (New York: St. Martin's Press, 1969).

3. Sharaf, *Fury*; Wilhelm Reich, *Passion of Youth: An Autobiography, 1897–1922*, ed. Mary Boyd Higgins and Chester M. Raphael, with translations by Philip Schmitz and Jerri Tompkins (New York: Farrar, Straus & Giroux, 1988).

4. Wilhelm Reich, *Wilhelm Reich: Early Writings*, trans. Philip Schmitz (New York: Farrar, Straus & Giroux, 1975), vol. 1, p. 66.

5. Ibid., p. 68

6. Ibid., pp. 68–69; Reich, *Passion of Youth*, p. 29.

7. Reich, *Passion of Youth*, p. 34.

8. Sharaf, *Fury*, p. 44.

9. Ibid., p. 52.

10. Richard F. Sterba, *Reminiscences of a Viennese Psychoanalyst* (Detroit: Wayne State University Press, 1982), p. 87.

11. Wilhelm Reich. *The Function of the Orgasm*, trans. Theodore P. Wolfe (New York: Meridian, 1970), p. 17.

12. Ibid., p. 7.

13. Ibid.

14. Wilhelm Reich, *Reich Speaks of Freud* (New York: Farrar, Straus & Giroux, 1967), p. 40.

15. Wilhelm Reich, *Genitality in the Theory and Therapy of Neurosis*, 2nd ed., trans. Philip Schmitz, ed. Mary Higgins and Chester M. Raphael (New York: Farrar, Straus & Giroux, 1980), p. 9.

16. Reich, *Function of the Orgasm*, p. 89.

17. Ibid., p. 63.

18. Ibid., p. 62.

19. Reich, *Genitality*, pp. 73–74.

20. Ibid., p. 75.

21. Reich, *Function of the Orgasm*, p. 100.

22. Ibid.

23. Ibid., p. 69

24. Ibid.

25. Ibid.

26. Ibid., p. 75.

27. Ibid., p. 79 (italics in the original).

28. Ibid., p. 106.

29. Sterba, *Reminiscences*, p. 31.

30. Ibid.

31. Reich, *Function of the Orgasm*, p. 101.

32. Sterba, *Reminiscences*, p. 36.

33. Ibid., p. 37.

34. Celia Bertin, *Marie Bonaparte: A Life* (New York: Harcourt Brace Jovanovich, 1982), p. 152.

35. Reich, *Function of the Orgasm*, p. 141.

36. Sterba, *Reminiscences*, p. 87.

37. Reich, *Function of the Orgasm*, p. 172 (italics in the original).

38. Ibid., p. 200.

39. Ibid., p. 201 (italics in the original).

40. Derek Freeman, *Margaret Mead and Samoa: The Making and Unmaking of an Anthropological Myth* (Cambridge, Mass.: Harvard University Press, 1983).

41. Bertin, *Marie Bonaparte*, p. 141.

42. Ibid., p. 147.

43. Ibid., p. 155.

44. Ibid., p. 157.

45. Ibid.

46. Ibid., p. 170.

47. Ibid., p. 175.

48. Hilda Doolittle, *Tribute to Freud* (New York: New Directions, 1974), p. 18 (italics in the original).

49. Wilhelm Reich, *People in Trouble* [vol. 2 of *The Emotional Plague of Mankind*], trans. Philip Schmitz (New York: Farrar, Straus & Giroux, 1976), pp. 135, 198–201.

50. Reich, *Function of the Orgasm*, pp. 239–240.

51. Ibid., pp. 241–242.

Chapter 4

Character
and Resistance

> The great boon of repression is that it makes it possible to
> live decisively in an overwhelmingly miraculous and incom-
> prehensible world.
>
> —Ernest Becker, *The Denial of Death*

Reich did not invent the psychoanalytic idea of character. In 1908, in "Character and Anal Eroticism," Freud identified
the anal character as exceptionally orderly, parsimonious, and
obstinate, qualities that he attributed to an anal zone during
childhood, "intensified in the innate sexual constitution of these
persons."[1] Freud speculated that "one ought to consider whether
other types of character do not also show a connection with the
excitability of particular erotogenic zones."[2]

Undoubtedly, Reich was also influenced by Adler, who, in an
acrimonious split with Freud, co-opted the study of character. In
1912, Adler posed a psychological theory of character development
in *The Nervous Character*, and in other papers he related organ
inferiority to neurotic character.[3] Reich found Adler disappointing.
"He scolded at Freud," Reich wrote. "Really, he, Adler, had
achieved it. The Oedipus complex, he said, was nonsense."[4]

In psychoanalytic circles, "character" and "sexuality" were
considered incompatible opposites, and "character" was not considered an appropriate topic of discussion in Freud's society.[5] Reich,
with his unerring instinct for the forbidden, managed to develop a

49

theory and technique around character that worked in harmony with his theory of genitality. He saw character as the rigid, constricted defense system that blocked the natural flow of energy.

Reich influenced the course of psychoanalysis in the 1920s. When he joined the Vienna Psychoanalytic Society in 1920, it was generally thought that a neurosis could be cured in three to six months. "Freud referred several patients to me with the notation, 'For psychoanalysis, impotence, three months.'"[6] With no concept of an overall character, psychoanalysts regarded neurotic symptoms as intruders in an otherwise healthy organism. Furthermore, there was no conviction yet that an analyst needed to be thoroughly analyzed. Reading Freud's writings and analyzing one's own dreams were considered sufficient. Max Eitington, for instance, had been analyzed in a few weeks by taking evening walks with Freud.

The goal of therapy appears to have been the reconstruction of central childhood traumas that, associated with Oedipal issues and castration fear, had triggered the neurotic symptoms. With the root cause revealed, the symptoms were supposed to wither away, which in fact they did in some cases. The therapeutic technique was therefore passive on the part of the therapist, who encouraged the patient in free association and dream analysis. There was little awareness of negative transference, and no system to investigate the technical aspects of therapy. By the 1920s, the emphasis on sexuality was downplayed. The relation of psychoanalysis to natural science remained obscure and undeveloped.

Reich had trouble with many of the psychoanalytic rules as his technique developed. Most analysts imposed sexual abstinence for the duration of treatment. "If that rule was imposed," Reich wrote, "how could the patients' genital disturbances be understood and eliminated?"[7] Reich took issue with the concept that the analyst should not be seen so that the patient would project his transference upon a blank screen: "This, instead of eliminating, confirmed in the patient the feeling of dealing with an 'invisible,' unapproachable, superhuman, that is, according to infantile thinking, a sexless being. How could the patient overcome his fear of sex which made him ill?"[8]

In 1925, Reich wrote *The Impulsive Character*, which appears to have been the first formulation of the borderline character.[9]

"These impulsive characters," he later wrote, "seemed to represent *a transitional stage from neurosis to psychosis.*"[10] Since Reich was treating a number of borderline personalities in the limited clinical environment, he would hardly have found the psychoanalytic techniques effective. His clients needed direct engagement with the therapist. Reich encouraged even greater contact, as he gained experience, by inviting his patients to criticize him. He wanted to be looked upon in an "unauthoritative, *human,* way."[11] He may have been influenced by Sándor Ferenczi, whom he greatly admired, who was known for his unorthodox, playful, interactive therapeutic style.

Reich suggested to Freud that a technical seminar be formed. Established in 1922, it was chaired by his boss at the clinic, Hitschmann. Reich also formed a seminar for the new members of the Society, providing a powerful counterforce to the subtle and not so subtle control of the old guard. In 1924, he took over the technical seminar and imposed a new system. "We discussed exclusively situations of resistance. Completely helpless at first, we soon began to learn a great deal."[12] The technical seminar dealt with latent hostility, negative transference, and eventually the appropriateness of interpretation before resistance had been addressed and resolved. Reich observed the defensive stance of the patient. Dissolving symptoms was insufficient. "Real cure could be achieved only through elimination of the characterological basis of the symptoms."[13]

All therapeutic efforts bounded back, as it were, from "a thick, hard wall." The patients were "armored" against any attack. There was no technique known in the literature that would shake this hardened surface. It was the whole character that resisted. With this I was at the beginning of character-analysis.[14]

In later years, Sterba enthusiastically recalled Reich's remarkable seminars. Reich's technical approach to resistances, he wrote, prepared the ground for Anna Freud's *Ego and the Mechanisms of Defense* (1936):

Reich had a particular sensitivity for the recognition of latent resistances and their often hardly noticeable influence on the patient's conscious material. The form in which the patient brought forth his material, his manner and his peculiarity of speech, how he entered the office, how he shook hands with the analyst (in Vienna an established custom at the beginning and closing of each session)— all this Reich taught us to use as important information, particularly about latent resistances. We students and younger members of the group gained tremendously from his insight into theory and technique in handling resistances.[15]

Psychoanalysis followed the rule that the therapist interpreted the material in the order in which it came up in the sessions, but Reich developed a vastly different rule. He dealt first with the immediate situation, the relationship of patient to therapist, and the resistance, the armoring, the thick, hard wall of character, before he interpreted repressed material.

After having maintained for some time that one should interpret resistance before the material, Reich suffered a setback in what became his classic confrontations with Freud. Perhaps the incident can be viewed as the way in which he challenged Freud:

In December 1926, in Freud's inner circle, I gave a talk on character-analytic technique. As the central problem I presented the question as to whether, in the presence of a latent negative attitude, one should interpret the patient's incestuous desires, or whether one would have to wait until the patient's distrust was eliminated. Freud interrupted me; Why would you *not* interpret the material in the order in which it appears? Of *course* one has to analyze and interpret incest dreams as soon as they appear. This I had not expected. I kept on substantiating my point of view. . . . My opponents in the seminar gloated and pitied me. I remained calm.[16]

In the mid-1920s, Sterba and his wife became friends with Reich and his wife Annie. They took walks and skied together. Sterba noticed toward the end of the decade that "Reich became more sadistic in 'hammering' at the patient's resistive armor. An increasing number of the members and trainees in the seminars could not follow him and had to contradict his technical advice, a fact that made him embittered and belligerent."[17] Sterba also found that Reich became more rigid in his technical approach, inhibiting the flexibility and open-mindedness of the analytic approach. His belligerence, according to Sterba, brought him into conflict with Freud: "Even Freud could not tolerate Reich's stubborn insistence on his being right. In one of the meetings in Freud's apartment which I attended, Freud stopped Reich's righteous repetition of his argument by not permitting him to continue his discussion."[18]

Reich became aware of this criticism of him in 1927. "In the Psychoanalytic Association at large, however," he wrote, "the mistaken interpretation of the ego-theory flourished more and more. The tension kept growing. Suddenly it was discovered that I was 'very aggressive' or that I was 'only riding my hobby' and was overemphasizing the significance of genitality."[19]

Reich was under terrible pressures in 1927. He was increasingly torn over political issues that his psychoanalytic colleagues in Vienna were able to ignore. With rejection from Freud on a number of issues, together with some physical illness, Reich became more self-protective and driven.

Reich drew up descriptions of different character types: impulsive, passive-feminine, aristocratic, hysterical, compulsive, phallic-narcissistic, and masochistic. He also made a general distinction between a neurotic character and a genital character, and he identified a mass character. Reich believed that man's antisocial impulses—his evil fantasies and expressions—were a rude husk that hid perfectly decent, simple human nature: "With the attainment of the capacity for full genital surrender, the whole being of the patients changed so rapidly and so basically that at first I could not understand it. It was difficult to see how the tenacious neurotic process could admit of such a sudden change."[20]

The patients, once changed, no longer accepted the moralistic attitude of the environment, nor could they continue to work mechanically. They looked for meaningful work and developed an ethical system that supported their inner nature. They developed a self-assurance based on sexual potency. Instead of abiding by moral regulation, they were self-regulated.

And so Reich saw that the therapeutic task was to change "neurotic character" into "genital character." But the task grew overwhelmingly large. Working at the clinic, Reich heard daily of overcrowded living conditions and sexual repression. The flood of damaged people perplexed him. Obviously, psychoanalysis could not begin to reverse the damage created by society through improper upbringing. Reich became committed to bringing psycho-analysis into a social framework. Freud, over seventy years old, in pain from successive operations on his jaw, protected by fame and recognition and a devoted following, might nod agreement over the young, militant Reich's concern for an all-out war on neurosis, but Freud was hardly in any condition to follow him in a fight against an authoritarian state.

Reich's politically oriented activities, assisting the Communist Party by developing sex clinics that disseminated information, began in the late 1920s and ended abruptly with Hitler's rise to power in 1933. By that time, Reich had brought his character-analysis to bear on the state of mind of the average citizen and published *The Mass Psychology of Fascism*, which made him something of an underground hero.[21]

Reich said that character structure was not restricted to capitalists: "It is prevalent among the working men of all occupations. There are liberal capitalists and reactionary workers. *There are no 'class distinctions' when it comes to character.*"[22] He saw that fascism was rooted in the authoritarian family, in particular the lower-middle-class family, which repressed sexuality and blindly pursued an ideology of duty and honor. Religious fear also helped to suppress and debilitate sexual expression:

> The man who attains genital satisfaction is honorable, responsible, brave, and controlled, without making much of a fuss about it. These attitudes are an organic part of his personality. The man whose genitals are weakened, whose sexual structure is full of contradictions, must continually remind himself to control his sexuality, to preserve his sexual dignity, to be brave in the face of temptations, etc.[23]

Reich believed that the authoritarian family system had devitalized its children so that they felt helpless and therefore easily identified with a "Führer" (leader). The wretchedness of their material surroundings was offset by the exalted idea of being members of a master race: "He eats poorly and insufficiently, but attaches great importance to a 'decent suit of clothes.' A silk hat and dress coat become the material symbol of this character structure."[24]

Reich saw the Church as shamelessly assisting in the development of the mass neurotic man by suppressing sexuality: "Children do not believe in God. It is when they have to learn to suppress the sexual excitation that goes hand in hand with masturbation that the belief in God generally becomes embedded in them. Owing to this suppression, they acquire a fear of pleasure."[25]

Reich was able to describe character from a psychoanalytic, a sociological, and a biological perspective. Throughout his professional life, Reich the natural scientist used images from nature to explain his work. He felt like "a worm in the universe."[26] With his lifelong incurable eczema, he may have developed an unconscious affinity with life forms whose vulnerability is apparent in the skin. A similar vulnerability was expressed in another image that evokes a sense of the exposed body. Toward the end of his life, in an interview in 1953, Reich told Kurt Eisler, the director of the Freud Archives, that he felt like a deer in an open meadow: "The pioneer is like a deer in the open meadow, and all his critics and all his enemies are all around him in the bushes. They can shoot from ambush and he can't do a thing about it."[27] Of his early days in psychoanalysis, as we saw in the last chapter, Reich described himself as a "shark in a pond of carps."[28] Expressing his pessimism about curing neurosis in adults, he said: "Once a tree has grown crooked, you can't straighten it out."[29] The image of the worm in the universe was not only about vulnerability but about insignificance, achievement, and withdrawal. Contained within the image was an observer who saw himself from a great height, his own internalized critical father, an observer who in his last years was written into his manuscripts as the silent observer:

> During the past twenty years, the difficulty of seeing one's finite, sharply delimited scientific work in terms of the infinity of life has been ever with me. In the background of all detailed work was always the feeling of being nothing but a worm in the universe. When one flies in an airplane above a highway at an altitude of a mile, the cars seem to be crawling along.[30]

The silent observer perhaps despaired at times of great achievement.

Later the observer moved from the "stage" of life to the "meadow" and, from the perspective of nature, observed the egoistic bickering of those caught on the world's stage. As egocentric as

55

others saw him, Reich, after the death of his parents and the loss of his home, undoubtedly observed himself from a great distance, sometimes in anguish, sometimes dramatically with a sense of romantic heroism, and sometimes in neutrality, in detachment, with an identification to nature as a whole, diminishing the importance of individual men. It was probably as the observer that Reich refused to defend himself when he came under attack from the press in Scandinavia and later in the United States. One might also say that "the silent observer" reflected a dangerous dissociation and withdrawal on Reich's part, since he only intensified his vulnerability by refusing to provide the simplest defense for himself.

Reich was fascinated by the movements of paramecia and amoebas. During the Berlin Psychoanalytic Congress in 1922, he was impressed when Freud compared the projection and retraction of psychic interest with the movement of pseudopodia in the amoeba. During that time, Reich was professionally identified with psychoanalysis and explained armor in Freud's terms of id and ego. Later he abandoned Freud's theoretical model for his own, based on a biological image:

> The ego, the part of the personality which is exposed to the outer world, is where character formation takes place; it is a buffer in the struggle between id and outer world. In the interest of self-preservation, the ego, attempting to mediate between the two sides, introjects the frustrating objects of the outer world which then form the super-ego.[31]

The organism, motivated by anxiety, erects a protective mechanism between itself and the outer world in what is to become a character formation. Reich used an image of the protozoa to explain his idea:

> One is reminded here of certain protozoa. There are many among them who protect themselves against the outer world by means of an armor of inorganic material. The motility of these armored protozoa is considerably restricted compared with the plain amoeba; the contact with the outer world is limited to the pseudopodia which can be put out through small openings in the armor and pulled back again.[32]

As a corollary to the concept of armor, Reich developed the concept of contact and contactlessness. After the most blatant defenses have been dissolved by an analysis, there remains a level of protectiveness that the patient refuses to relinquish, described by Reich as psychic contactlessness: "When patients feel themselves to be strange, unrelated, and lacking interest, it is because of this conflict between an object-libidinal tendency and the tendency to flee back into the self."[33] The balance of opposing forces creates the apparent passivity and lack of contact. Reich worked, for instance, with a patient who, behind his passive-feminine attitude, maintained a lack of contact with people: "The patient himself had no immediate awareness of this; on the contrary, his passive-feminine tendency to lean on others deceived him about it and gave him the feeling that he had especially intensive relations with the outer world."[34]

Reich's most powerful and fruitful image related to the amoeba and the worm was the bladder, from which he was to derive a new representation for armoring. Until blocked, energy expanded toward the world and the periphery and contracted away from the world toward the core in a natural pulsation. The bladder image described the physical dilemma of all armor, but in particular the dilemma of masochism.

Reich could never make sense of Freud's death instinct, and felt that there was no clinical justification for it. The clients who were failing in therapy to whom the death instinct was attributed eventually provoked an alternative theory, Reich's concept of masochism. With one client who begged Reich to beat him, Reich finally complied, hitting him with a ruler. Rather than enjoying the pain, his patient merely endured it in order to break the body tension, to experience release. Reich saw the body as a taut bladder: "The patients complain about being taut, filled up, as if they were going to burst, to explode. . . . They dread any loosening of their armor."[35] Around 1929, Reich saw that the psychic conflict between sexual pleasure and moral restriction is enacted physically through muscular spasm. Whereas in a genitally healthy organism sexual release is full and convulsive, in the masochistic structure release is impossible. Energy expanding is sexual and pleasurable, but in contraction it is experienced as anxiety:

How would a bladder behave if it were blown up with air from the inside and could not burst? . . . The bladder, if it could express itself in its state of insoluble tension, would complain. In its help-lessness, it would look for the causes of its suffering on the outside, and would be reproachful. . . .

The neurotic patient has become rigid at the body periphery, at the same time having retained his "central" vitality with its demands. He is not at ease "within his own skin," he is "inhibited," "unable to realize himself," "hemmed in" as if by a wall; he "lacks contact," he feels "tight enough to burst." He strives with all his might "towards the world" but he is "tied down."[36]

The bladder, Reich thought, extends out in the form of a worm or an intestine, can execute rhythmical movements in its expansion and contraction, and can discharge built-up energy with a few con-tractions, or the whole body might make a motion like a snake. Or indeed, as in cell division, a bladder, by division into two blad-ders, can maintain the same volume while being surrounded by a larger, less taut membrane, a process of relaxation. For Reich, con-tractions to release built-up energy represented the orgasm reflex.

By the 1940s, Reich had grown tired of words in therapy. He had come to see the life beneath the parade of ego. The bladder, a circle, freed Reich from the images of psychoanalysis, from ego and id. As an ancient symbol of wholeness, the circle became Reich's model of the self. For Reich, the circle, suggesting the amoeba and the bladder image, expressed the three layers: the peripheral or polite superficial layer; the secondary layer of armor, the habitat of the devil and antisocial impulses; and the core layer where matter-of-fact, decent human nature resides.

As he grew older, Reich became more of a seer. "The living functions autonomously," he wrote, "beyond the realms of language, intellect, or volition."[37] The expression of the armored individual is of "holding back," whereas the unarmored individual is able to give, be present, and surrender to the partner in sexual embrace. Reich saw the living energy beneath the armor, beneath the defensive chatter. He became one who saw always the inner, natu-ral man in others: "If one lets the patient talk at random, one will find that the talking leads away from the problems, that it obscures them. . . . For as soon as the patient ceases to talk, the bodily expression of emotion becomes clearly manifest."[38]

Notes

1. Sigmund Freud, *Collected Papers*, vol. 2 (London: Hogarth Press, 1950), p. 46.

2. Ibid., p. 50.

3. See Paul E. Stepansky, *In Freud's Shadow: Adler in Context* (Hillsdale, N.J.: Analytic Press, 1983), p. 151.

4. Wilhelm Reich, *The Function of the Orgasm*, trans. Theodore P. Wolfe (New York: Meridian, 1970), p. 17.

5. Ibid., p. 51.

6. Ibid., p. 31.

7. Ibid., p. 146.

8. Ibid., p. 147.

9. Wilhelm Reich, *The Impulsive Character and Other Writings*, trans. Barbara G. Koopman (New York: New American Library, 1974).

10. Ibid., p. 57 (italics in the original).

11. Ibid., p. 147 (italics in the original).

12. Ibid., p. 95.

13. Ibid., p. 125.

14. Ibid., p. 114.

15. Richard F. Sterba, *Reminiscences of a Viennese Psychoanalyst* (Detroit: Wayne State University Press, 1982), p. 35.

16. Reich, *Function of the Orgasm*, p. 142.

17. Sterba, *Reminiscences*, p. 87.

18. Ibid.

19. Reich, *Function of the Orgasm*, p. 105.

20. Ibid., p. 149.

21. Ilse Ollendorff Reich, *Wilhelm Reich: A Personal Biography* (New York: St. Martin's Press, 1969), p. 33.

22. Wilhelm Reich, *The Mass Psychology of Fascism*, trans. Vincent R. Carfagno (New York: Farrar, Straus & Giroux, 1970), p. xxiv (italics in the original).

23. Ibid., p. 55.

24. Ibid., p. 47.

25. Ibid., p. 150.

26. Reich, *Function of the Orgasm*, p. 22.

27. Wilhelm Reich, *Reich Speaks of Freud* (New York: Farrar, Straus & Giroux, 1967), p. 101.

28. Ibid., p. 40.

29. Ibid., p. 70.

30. Reich, *Function of the Orgasm*, p. 22.

31. Wilhelm Reich, *Character Analysis*, 3rd ed., trans. Theodore P. Wolfe

(New York: Farrar, Straus & Giroux, 1949), p. 159.
32. Ibid., pp. 159–160.
33. Ibid., p. 319.
34. Ibid., p. 317.
35. Reich, *Function of the Orgasm*, p. 228.
36. Ibid., pp. 231–232 (italics in the original).
37. Reich, *Character Analysis*, p. 365.
38. Ibid., p. 362.

Chapter 5

Jung, Psychopathology, and the Individuation Process

Be not afeard: the isle is full of noises,
Sounds and sweet airs that give delight and hurt not.
Sometimes a thousand twangling instruments
Will hum about mine ears; and sometimes voices
That, if I then had waked after long sleep,
Will make me sleep again. And then, in dreaming,
The clouds methought would open and show riches
Ready to drop upon me, that when I waked,
I cried to dream again.

—Caliban, *The Tempest*

In writing about Jung and psychopathology, one is faced with an apparent contradiction, because Jung's intention, in his professional maturity, was to build a system of thought around the healthy evolving human being. Jung criticized the Freudian and Adlerian systems because they reflected an overemphasis on neurotic states of mind:

Both schools, to my way of thinking, deserve reproach for overemphasizing the pathological aspect of life and for interpreting man too exclusively in the light of his defects. . . . For my part, I prefer to look at man in the light of what in him is healthy and sound, and to free the sick man from that point of view, which colors every page Freud has written. Freud's teaching is definitely one-sided in that it generalizes from facts that are relevant only to neurotic states of mind; its validity is really confined to those states. . . . In any case, Freud's is not a psychology of the healthy mind.[1]

Jung's view of psychopathology had several origins. In his early work as a doctor, before the evolution of his own theories, he treated a severely disturbed hospitalized population. His studies of psychosis and neurosis made positive references to Freud.[2] The basic definitions developed in his early career remained relatively unchanged throughout his life. He developed the concept of the complex, which became rooted in the basic language of psychoanalytic thought. But in his theoretical development, Jung moved into what we might now term a holistic point of view around emotional disturbance:

More and more we turn our attention from the visible disease and direct it upon the man as a whole. We have come to understand that psychic suffering is not a definitely localized, sharply delimited phenomenon, but rather the symptom of a wrong attitude assumed by the total personality. We can therefore not hope for a thorough cure to result from a treatment restricted to the trouble itself, but only from a treatment of the personality as a whole.[3]

Jung's statement is parallel to Reich's concept of character, which could be summarized as a total bodily attitude of the organism.

Jung began his professional career in 1900 in Burghölzli Mental Hospital in Zurich under the tutelage of Eugen Bleuler. Twenty-five years old, Jung had entered a field of science that had little promise according to his colleagues, and had turned down an enviable assistantship in internal medicine with one of his teachers. Mental illness was regarded as having little relationship to normal life. The hospital was set aside from the city's busy commercial life, as were the doctors, who lived with the patients and were, through association, excluded from the "normal" world. Schizophrenia—or dementia praecox, as it was called then—was considered physiologically caused and irreversible. A patient who recovered through treatment or lack of treatment was viewed as never having been truly schizophrenic.

Jung began a study of schizophrenia using the association test. A list of commonplace words was read to the subject, who was asked to associate or respond to the word spontaneously, without reflection. The subject's responses were timed and an average time established, so that variations from the mean could be noted. Jung's work with the association test fit easily into the context of the more progressive investigative clinical scholarship of his time, which found the bizarre verbal behavior of schizophrenic patients fascinating.

Erwin Stransky studied the spontaneous thought associations of normal subjects when their attention was relaxed. In his experiment, he asked his subjects to talk randomly for one minute without paying attention to what they said.[4] The use of language, the perseverations and contaminations, were comparable to the verbal productions of schizophrenics. The relaxation or "lowering" of attention was referred to by a number of phrases, such as "apperceptive deterioration" or "apperceptive weakness," or by the term that Jung eventually settled on, Pierre Janet's *"abaissement du niveau mental"* (lowering of the mental level). According to Janet, Jung wrote, "dissociation was the result of the 'abaissement du niveau mental' which destroys the hierarchy and promotes, or actually causes, the formation of automatism."[5] Emil Kraepelin noticed, as well, the similarity between the language of dreams and the language of schizophrenia.[6]

In his first seven years at Burghölzli, Jung studied Freud's remarkable *Interpretation of Dreams* and compared Freud's work on hysteria to the mechanisms underlying schizophrenia. Kraepelin had noted what he called "emotional deterioration" in schizophrenia, and Stransky had speculated about the lack of coordination between the emotional content and the "ideational content dominating the psyche at the time."[7] From these studies and many others, Jung formulated the theory that the behavior of schizophrenia could be explained through the concept of the complex. With the *"abaissement du niveau mental,"* the cause of which was uncertain, an inattention or weakening of ego-dominance allowed the emergence of complexes that were feeling-toned ideas, representative of conflicts that had previously occurred, minor or major traumas to the psychic and somatic life. These complexes represented disharmonies in the psyche and interrupted the flow of conscious life:

> The ego itself was a complex. The ego is the psychological expression of the firmly associated combination of all body sensations. One's own personality is therefore the firmest and strongest complex, and (good health permitting) it weathers all psychological storms.[8]

Jung graphically described how the body incorporates psychic trauma into its overall functioning. His work with the association test and the galvanic skin test alerted him to the way in which the psyche and the body interrelate, an awareness that he never lost. But it was Reich's genius to insist on this connection when Freud was following a somewhat contrary rule. Freud insisted on following psychological aspects to the end, rather than being distracted by neurological details. He wanted his new science to blossom and not to be sidetracked into somatic explanations.

As an example of psychic trauma, Jung explained, we can imagine someone severely frightened by a dog. The experience is accompanied by muscle tensions and various reactions of the sympathetic nervous system. Innumerable body sensations are altered, and, perhaps for months afterward, fleeting memories of the incident reawaken the experience, which is partially relived. In time, the terror-complex, rather than being integrated, is submerged. It surfaces briefly, however, whenever, for subtle and varied reasons, the experience is retriggered. In the case of neurosis, the complex has become, to some degree, autonomous and vies for dominance with the ego, but the struggle of the ego against the unconscious intruder remains:

> Thought and action are constantly disturbed and distorted by a strong complex, in large things and small. The ego-complex is, so to say, no longer the whole of the personality; side by side with it there exists another being, living its own life and hindering and disturbing the development of the ego-complex, for the symptomatic actions often take up a good deal of time and energy at its expense.[9]

With schizophrenia, the cohesiveness of the psyche is no longer merely strained but finally shattered. The ego-complex has lost dominance, and other complexes rule at will. The difference between neurosis and psychosis is seen as a matter of degree. Jung later recorded that when he left Burghölzli in 1909 to pursue a busy private practice, he thought he would no longer encounter schizophrenics. To his surprise, he found many who had avoided the hospital and maintained themselves through visits to psychotherapists. He also rather frequently encountered neurotic patients who harbored latent psychoses. Neurotic defenses sometimes defended against a more global destruction of the ego-complex.

In 1907, Jung published "The Psychology of Dementia Praecox,"[10] in which he reviewed the relevant literature and discussed his use of the association test to establish and identify complexes in his schizophrenic patients. His use of this associative tool was scientific but also highly intuitive and at times uncanny. Jung's association test indicated the nature and presence of complexes in normal as well as neurotic and psychotic patients. Psychopathology resulted when a complex that was present in normal people was sufficiently able to dominate over the ego-complex and to create severe disturbance. The concept of the complex remained with Jung as a foundation of his understanding of psychopathology.

After 1907, when Jung began his personal association with Freud, his scientific work rapidly led him to conclusions outside the mainstream of scholarship—investigations that ultimately alienated Freud himself. We might view the growing theoretical differences between Freud and Jung as a result, in part, of their different patient populations. Freud worked with neurotics exclusively, whereas Jung, at least until 1909, worked predominantly with schizophrenics.

For Jung, the unconscious material that erupted in the therapy session from the schizophrenic patient was markedly different from the unconscious material presented in therapy by the neurotic patient. Jung came to feel that beneath the thin layer of a personal unconscious (a small, individual storehouse of private associations) lies a vast associative connection to mankind, a universal mythic world that relates to the folklore and the racial history of humanity. Such material, Jung concluded, is not effectively understood as the contents of a personal unconscious, as Freud believed; interpreted as material from the personal unconscious alone, there is neither therapeutic response nor results.

For Freud, therapeutic resolution was in the commitment to rational containment, through the confessional aspects of the cathartic method, and through analysis of childhood experiences. Reference to the larger issues of myth had value, but myth was better reduced to rational statement. For Jung, however, symbolic meaning was not necessarily to be translated. Dreams were not symbolic disguises, as they were for Freud. In a letter to a "Dr. N.," Jung wrote: "You shouldn't interpret the symbols produced by dreams reductively, but must understand them as true symbols, that is, as the best possible formulation for unknown facts that cannot be reduced to anything else."[11]

Jung saw symbols, myths, fairy tales, and dreams as the best expression for what they described. They were not unnecessary intrusions into the normal world of reason, but expressions of what had directed the psychic energy of man throughout the ages. For Jung, the intrusion into consciousness of this material was not legitimately reduced to its sexual content alone:

> It was this frequent reversion to archaic forms of an association found in schizophrenia that first gave me the idea of an unconscious not consisting only of originally conscious contents that have been lost, but having a deeper layer of the same universal character as the mythological motifs which typify human fantasy in general. These motifs are not *invented* so much as *discovered*; they are typical forms that appear spontaneously all over the world, independently of tradition, in myths, fairy-tales, fantasies, dreams, visions, and the delusional systems of the insane. On closer investigation they prove to be typical attitudes, modes of action—thought processes and impulses which must be regarded as constituting the instinctive behavior typical of the human species. The term I chose for this, namely "archetype," therefore coincides with the biological concept of the "pattern of behavior." In no sense is it a question of inherited ideas, but of inherited instinctive impulses and forms that can be observed in all living creatures.[12]

According to Jung, the schizophrenic is so inundated with archetypal material from the collective unconscious that the patient is unable to integrate it successfully. Jung cites an example at Burghölzli that led to his concept of the collective unconscious: "I once came across the following hallucination in a schizophrenic patient: he told me he could see an erect phallus on the sun. When he moved his head from side to side, he said, the sun's phallus moved with it, and *that was where the wind came from.*"[13]

In 1910, while immersed in mythological studies, he came across a Mithraic liturgy that included instructions, invocations, and visions. To his surprise, one of those visions was: "And likewise the so-called tube, the origin of the ministering wind, for you will see hanging down from the disc of the sun something that looks like a tube."[14]

Jung, whose interests were intense and varied, was well-equipped to deal with the myth and its implications. From childhood on, he had been interested in biology and archaeology. Working with schizophrenics, he had learned to identify the various subpersonalities, and he saw through dream analysis the various mythic themes that dominated his clients' inner lives. Eventually he was to ask of himself, "What myth am *I* living?" and move from considerations of psychopathology to issues of individuation or self-realization.[15] He saw man in general as having a collective consciousness rather than a truly developed individuality. Often an illusion of individuality is supported by the presence of what he called the persona, a mask established as an intermediary between oneself and the world; that is, the persona is one's presumed role in the world.[16] Jung came to feel that to be fully human the individual needs to differentiate himself or herself from the various complexes and archaic collective contents assumed to be the self. Through dream analysis and a process he called "active imagination," whereby in a waking state one actively engages the various inner personalities, one carries out the differentiation process.

The division between the sick and the normal was no longer a clear line, and the therapeutic process could be continued beyond the point of "adequate functioning." If Jung had been able to keep his investigations of pathology objectively focused outside himself, his major work would have ended with the association test and the complex, or perhaps it would have developed further in that vein. But Jung explored his relationships with his patients and investigated his own inner processes. Psychotherapy was in its infancy, transference was an untried concept, and Jung made no claim to objectivity. All that he had written, he said, was no more than a "subjective confession."[17] But more than any other psychologist, he made that subjective confession known to the public, in *Memories, Dreams, Reflections*.[18]

In later life, Jung displayed a greater capacity than Reich to protect himself, to stay hidden; and even with all his autobiographical confessions, he remains an exceedingly difficult man to know. For that reason, his early indiscretions and conflicts provide us with a sense of genuine engagement. There were ways in which Jung was not able to protect himself, and his notable victories were not won without spilling real blood. His investigations into his own nature and the nature of transference, as well as his fascination with madness, led him into deep involvements with patients that inevitably extended past professional boundaries. His willingness to open his heart created problems.

For example, Jung worked to cure an attractive, bright Russian girl, Sabina Spielrein, continuing the relationship for an extended period because, as he claimed in a letter to Freud, she needed extended support in recovery. In this case, he suffered from the depth of his commitment to her and his entrapment in the transference. Jung maintained in his letter to Freud that, contrary to Sabina's claims, she was never his mistress. According to her diary and letters, however, Jung, still inexperienced in a new field, fell in love with her and was decidedly indiscreet.[19] Jung wrote to Freud:

> She was, so to speak, my test case, for which reason I remembered her with special gratitude and affection. Since I knew from experience that she would immediately relapse if I withdrew my support, I prolonged the relationship over the years and in the end found myself morally obliged, as it were, to devote a large measure of friendship to her, until I saw that an unintended wheel had started turning, whereupon I finally broke with her. She was, of course, systematically planning my seduction, which I considered inopportune. Now she is seeking revenge.[20]

Bruno Bettelheim is of the opinion that Sabina Spielrein was not only Jung's lover but also a critical factor in the development of his concepts of the shadow and the anima. Spielrein was not acknowledged as an influence either by Jung or by Freud, whose concept of the death instinct was developed from her earlier work. In a later letter to Freud, dated June 21, 1909, Jung acknowledged some guilt regarding the Spielrein relationship: "I nevertheless deplore the sins I have committed, for I am largely to blame." He also acknowledged that "my action was a piece of knavery."[21] Sabina's mother received an anonymous letter warning her of Jung's compromising relationship, and Bettelheim speculates that Jung's departure from Burghölzli in March 1909 was to avoid the possibility of further scandal.[22] Whether Jung's love affair with Sabina was acted out sexually is not clear.[23] It does appear, however, that he loved her with some passion.

In time, the relationship found a new balance, and Sabina received her medical degree and became an analyst and teacher. Jung's extended involvement with Sabina was later repeated with Toni Wolff, who had also been his patient. Both women, of exceptional intelligence, intimately knew from their own struggles the process of inner healing. Perhaps they were able to provide an intellectual companionship and validation otherwise lacking in Jung's life. Later, when he was in the throes of his personal trial by fire, his own confrontation with the unconscious, Toni was able to anchor him sufficiently with her sensitive awareness so that he could come to terms with the anima—the unleashed, unknown feminine in himself. Over time, Emma Jung was able to accept Toni, acknowledging that without her assistance at a critical time, her husband might have become psychotic.

A model that Jung discovered later in alchemy explains the process he engaged in with these special women. The alchemical work involves a marriage between a king and queen, the masculine and feminine within oneself, enacted by the alchemist and a female assistant. In his concept of transference, Jung described how in the deepest work both the therapist and the patient are "in the soup." Both are transformed by the relationship. The therapist is not immune. Each partner must learn to distinguish between the projected self and the partner who stands outside them.

While still in Burghölzli, Jung gave himself over passionately to the cure of Otto Gross. He became close friends with Gross and his wife, but failed to cure him after untold hours of work. In June 1908, Jung wrote to Freud:

> In spite of everything he is my friend, for at bottom he is a very good and fine man with an unusual mind. He is now living under

the delusion that I have cured him. . . .

    I don't know with what feelings you will receive this news. For me this experience is one of the harshest in my life, for in Gross I discovered many aspects of my own nature, so that he often seemed like my twin brother—but for the Dementia praecox. This is tragic. You can guess what powers I have summoned up in myself in order to cure him. But in spite of the sorrow of it, I would not have missed this experience for anything; for in the end it has given me, with the help of a unique personality, a unique insight into the nethermost depths of Dementia pr.[24]

The price of Jung's involvement was high, and he had moments of bitterness. "Gross and Spielrein are bitter experiences," he wrote to Freud. "To none of my patients have I extended so much friendship, and from none have I reaped so much sorrow."[25]

    A further shocking incident in Jung's early career was the suicide of his talented young assistant, Honegger, who quietly injected himself with morphine. "The sole motive," Jung told Freud, "was to avoid a psychosis, for he did not under any circumstances want to give up living in accordance with the pleasure principle."[26] François Roustang feels that Jung's young assistant, so useful to Jung in secondary ways, was deeply affected by Jung's demands upon him. His suicide was entangled in Jung's life far more than is indicated by Jung's letter. It was not that Jung was so responsible as that he was unaware.[27]

    Through Gross, Jung was able to get a glimpse of himself in madness, and he sensed the depth of his own depression and inner disarray. His relationship with others had not been uniformly even. His relationship with Bleuler appears to have cooled as Jung's fondness for Freud developed. His relationship with Freud was fraught with unconscious fears and unresolved longing. His efforts with Gross were defeated by Gross, who appeared to be angry and competitive with Jung. His relationship with his wife, Emma, was in some ways lacking, since he apparently did not find her able to escort him in his deepest psychic wanderings. His relationship with Sabina was obscured and compromised through his own unconscious involvement, and he may have had reason to fear for his reputation. Under extreme psychological pressure, he appears to have lied and bullied his way through with Sabina and her inquiring mother. While such a picture does not endear us to Jung, we are better able to see the man who was finally to break down in 1913 and withdraw from the world for a while.

Jung's break with Freud was a gradual and crushing disappointment to both men. Probably they were never in full agreement from the beginning of their association in 1907, and their enormous investment in the professional friendship drew them into complex transference issues that exposed these private, cautious men far more than they intended. In *Dire Mastery*, François Roustang outlines the parry and thrust of their relationship in remarkable detail, pieced together from their letters. In a more general statement, he outlines the dilemma between them:

> Freud was looking for a brilliant pupil and not for a brilliant future leader. Jung was looking for an understanding father and not for a master who was eagerly looking for a successor to preserve the inheritance. Each man mistook the other, and this led to an endless crisscrossing back and forth between them which they both ignored or hid as well as or as poorly as they could. For years Freud wanted to believe, against all evidence, that Jung would accept his sexual theories, but it did worry him: "I believe it would be good policy for us to share the work in accordance with our characters and positions. . . . But I beg of you, don't sacrifice anything essential for the sake of pedagogic tact and affability, and don't deviate too far from me when you are really so close to me, for if you do, we may be played off against one another." Freud's obstinacy was not soon exhausted, since he was still convinced in January 1911 that Jung was "the man of the future." He was to lose all hope, apparently, only when the *Wandlungen* [Symbols of Transformation] came out; Freud was totally unable to write to Jung about it for a long time.[28]

It was not at all clear that psychoanalysis had any effect on schizophrenia. Jung held to his own research methods with a desperate passion. Freud had little understanding of dementia praecox but plenty of his own reference points to paranoia. Roustang explains their opposition in terms of their identification with dementia praecox and paranoia:

> Of course, Freud is not clinically a paranoic, no more than Jung is a schizophrenic. But their opposition is deeply rooted in these two types of knowledge (and madness). Each has to accomplish the difficult task of preserving himself both through and from his own

form of psychosis: to protect oneself with a theory and to protect oneself from madness by driving the other mad.[29]

For Jung, the reduction to sexual interpretation was superficial and boring. He naturally gravitated to the hidden symbol. Their styles were quite different. Roustang comments:

> What definitely differentiates paranoia from schizophrenia is that schizophrenia has no system of expulsion. It moves continuously from one element to the other without excluding or privileging anything. The paranoic never stops choosing and eliminating, whereas for the schizophrenic, who is indifferent to the isolated object, everything is readily interchangeable.[30]

With the publication of *Symbols of Transformation* in 1912, the relationship for all intents and purposes was over. In the eighth chapter, "The Sacrifice," Jung finally made painfully clear his incompatibility with Freudian theory. Jung's sense of libido extended far beyond the sexual, and he also argued with Freud's concept of the incest taboo:

> Therefore it cannot have been the incest taboo that forced mankind out of the original psychic state of non-differentiation. On the contrary, it was the evolutionary instinct peculiar to man, which distinguishes him so radically from all other animals and forced upon him countless taboos, among them the incest taboo. Against this "other urge" the animal in us fights with all his instinctive conservatism and misoneism—hatred of novelty—which are the two outstanding features of the primitive and feebly conscious individual. Our mania for progress represents the inevitable morbid compensation.[31]

Freud's theory, Jung said, sought the cause of neurosis in the remote past, a comfortable concept for the neurotic; but neurosis is recreated every day, a concept in harmony with Reich's view of character:

> Freud makes his theory of neurosis—so admirably suited to the nature of neurotics—much too dependent on the neurotic ideas from which precisely the patients suffer. This leads to the presence (which suits the neurotic down to the ground) that the *causa efficiens* of his neurosis lies in the remote past. In reality the neurosis is

Jung, Psychopathology, and the Individuation Process

manufactured anew every day, with the help of a false attitude that consists in the neurotic's thinking and feeling as he does and justifying it by his theory of neurosis.[32]

Regression goes back, said Jung, to a deeper level than the sexual, to a nutritive and digestive function, and then the libido withdraws into an intrauterine, prenatal condition, past the personal layer, into the collective psyche in a journey of the underworld. While the libido, immersed in the unconscious, triggers infantile reactions and fantasies, it also enlivens archetypal images that can have healing value:

> What actually happens in these incest and womb fantasies is that the libido immerses itself in the unconscious, thereby provoking infantile reactions, affects, opinions, and attitudes from the personal sphere, but at the same time activating collective images (archetypes) which have a compensatory and curative meaning such as have always pertained to the myth.[33]

Lou Andreas-Salomé, who was studying with Freud at the time, while appreciative of Jung's amplifications of the incest concept, felt that this attempt to make the libido concept all-inclusive was "naive philosophizing." In her journal of November 7, 1912, she wrote an insightful observation concerning the Freud-Jung dispute: "One is sometimes led to suspect that a quarrel over terms results when the real issue is much deeper and not a terminological one at all."[34] Present at the Munich Congress in early September 1913, she provided a unique if unflattering portrait of Jung at that time:

> At the congress the Zurich members sat at their own table opposite Freud's. Their behavior towards Freud can be characterized in a word; it is not so much that Jung diverges from Freud, as that he does it in such a way as if he had taken it on himself to rescue Freud and his cause by these divergences. If Freud takes up the lance to defend himself, it is misconstrued to mean that he cannot show scientific tolerance, is dogmatic, and so forth. One glance at the two of them tells which is the more dogmatic, the more in love with power. Two years ago Jung's booming laughter gave voice to a kind of robust gaiety and exuberant vitality, but now his earnestness is composed of pure aggression, ambition, and intellectual

73

brutality. I have never felt so close to Freud as here; not only on account of this break with his "son" Jung, whom he had loved and for whom he had practically transferred his cause to Zurich, but on account of the manner of the break—as though Freud had caused it by his narrow-minded obstinacy. Freud was the same as ever, but it was only with difficulty that he restrained his deep emotion; and there was nowhere I would have preferred to sit than right by his side.[35]

Brilliant, concerned for his reputation, driven in his work, caught in powerful relationships, enraged and injured, Jung lost credibility and friends when he cut himself loose from Freud. Alone on a train journey in October 1913, he saw in a vision a monstrous flood full of bodies covering Europe, a flood that turned to blood. He did not think of it as prophetic, but thought instead that he must prepare to be flooded by the contents of the unconscious, and there was little he could do about it. Approaching his own psychosis heroically, he prepared to record the event; he would keep careful notes, which might later be useful to science. Nine months later, while he was lecturing in Scotland, war broke out in Europe, a war that took practically everyone by surprise, since Western civilization had not been thinking about war for some time. Jung was shocked by the advent of war, but was profoundly relieved that his vision referred to events outside himself.

After the break with Freud, Jung began a period of inner uncertainty and disorientation, during which he used his technique of analysis and differentiation on himself:

I felt totally suspended in mid-air, for I had not yet found my own footing. . . . About this time I experienced a movement of unusual clarity to which I looked back over the way I had traveled so far. I thought, "Now you possess a key to mythology and are free to unlock all the gates of the unconscious psyche." But then something whispered within me, "Why open all gates?" And promptly the question arose of what, after all, I had accomplished. I had explained the myths of peoples of the past; I had written a book about the hero, the myth in which man has always lived. But in what myth does man live nowadays? In the Christian myth, the answer might be, "Do you live in it?" I asked myself. To be honest, the answer was no. For me, it is not what I live by. "Then do we no longer have any myth?" "No, evidently we no longer have any myth." "But then what is your myth—the myth in which you do live?" At this point the dialogue with myself became uncomfortable, and I stopped thinking. I had reached a dead end.[36]

Jung's identification with the hero died with his investigations, and he learned not to identify with the archetypal forces that spring up in us. Nietzsche, Jung felt, had identified with the prophetic voice that spoke so powerfully in *Thus Spake Zarathustra*, and that identification of the ego with Zarathustra corrupted his capacity to differentiate himself and contributed to his madness. Jung's intense inner processes made academic life entirely unpalatable, and with some anguish he withdrew from teaching. He continued to work with a few patients, but in working with them he put aside theories and rules and "simply helped the patients to understand the dreams' images by themselves, without applications of rules and theories."[37] Jung became more neutral, more an observer within himself without so much to defend. He learned from Philemon—one of his unconscious personalities, who had become a teacher to him—an unnerving and remarkable truth: that he was not the creator of the unconscious figures that peopled his life. Since in Western culture one assumes that inner experiences are unreal, Jung's stability was threatened as he experienced a contradictory vision of reality that he might otherwise view as psychotic.

In *Psychological Types*, Jung was able to create a larger context in which to view Freud's methods. The struggle between them did not end in 1913. If in Freud's world Jung was discounted as an unscientific mystic, in Jung's world Freud's extroverted thinking system could be contained as a single, restricted aspect of a larger approach. Jung distinguished two attitude types, introvert and extrovert:

> The introvert's attitude is an abstracting one; at bottom, he is always intent on withdrawing libido from the object, as though he had to prevent the object from gaining power over him. The extrovert, on the contrary, has a positive relation to the object. He affirms its importance to such an extent that his subjective attitude is constantly related to and oriented by the object.[38]

Four functions represent basic ways in which we each structure and interact with the world: feeling, thinking, sensation, and intuition. The two attitude types and four functions create eight personality types. Thus, a person may be either introverted or extroverted in his functioning. A person's first function represents a predominant mode of functioning. A second function may be well developed but secondary. The third function is in shadow but available to us. The fourth function represents the most primitive, undifferentiated side, an area where we are most blind, vulnerable, and unconscious. Since the functions are arranged in polarities, sensation is opposite intuition, and thinking is opposite feeling. Hence, the development of thinking as a first function relegates feeling to the fourth function. An introverted intuitive would have as his fourth function extroverted sensation.

Jung realized that he need no longer be a passive observer of his unconscious but that he could actively step into fantasy. He could hold on to a figure in a fantasy and demand something through active imagination. He launched out upon the sea of the unconscious as if in a sailing ship, aware of the awesome power, the very great risk involved.

In one such adventure, he found himself in a remote valley, evidently inhabited by primitives. A tall medicine man stood beside him. Seeing a somewhat illegible inscription in rock, Jung took hammer and chisel and sharpened the letters so that he could read it. The medicine man complained that a splinter had gotten in his eye and requested that Jung remove it. Jung agreed to do so only if the medicine man translated the inscription for him, which he did, explaining the meaning of the entire fantasy.[39]

Some years later, von Franz pointed out to Jung a story in the *Odyssey* that illustrated the process of active imagination. In the fourth book of the epic, Menelaus, becalmed on an island, having offended the gods in some way, meets, while walking on the sands, a beautiful woman, Eidothee, the daughter of Proteus, the Old Man of the Sea. She tells him how to get the information he wants from Proteus, who knows everything Menelaus needs to know. By catching Proteus asleep with his herd of seals, Menelaus is to hold him down and not let him go until he has told him what he needs. With four men, Menelaus holds Proteus down; but the old man goes through a number of transformations, becoming in turn a lion, a snake, a panther, a great boar, running water, and a great tree. Eventually, however, he tires, and Menelaus is able to learn what he needs.[40] In other words, as we attend to our inner images through active imagination, they change shape and dissolve as if to escape us. But through persistence we can eventually learn what we need.

Toward the end of his unconscious struggles, Jung spontaneously began each day by drawing mandalas, which brought him a sense of connection and relief from internal pressure, a process he was to study in great depth later. Like Reich, Jung developed powerful nonverbal ways of healing that reached to the depths of psychic life:

> Philemon and other figures of my fantasies brought home to me the crucial insight that there are things in the psyche which I do not produce, but which produce themselves and have their own life. Philemon represented a force which was not myself. In my fantasies I held conversations with him, and he said things which I had not consciously thought. For I observed clearly that it was he who spoke, not I. He said I treated thoughts as if I generated them myself, but in his view thoughts were like animals in the forest, or people in a room, or birds in the air, and added, "If you should see people in a room, you would not think that you had made those people, or that you were responsible for them." It was he who taught me psychic objectivity, the reality of the psyche.[41]

Mechanistic thinking of the nineteenth century discounted the entire internal process of feeling experience; it saw no sense in psychosis, nor in any irrationality, and viewed subjective experience as a dangerous indulgence, or, at best, a necessary evil. Subjectivity was something indulged in by women and children, and was viewed as charming but meaningless and inferior. For Jung, therefore, who had expressed such an overpowering masculine character, his precipitous descent into the subjective and internal reflected at least his partial acceptance and integration of the feminine within himself and a release from a narrowly power-oriented male ethos of the culture. His publication of *Psychological Types* (1921) legitimized the introverted and the intuitive outlook as different from, rather than inferior to, the extroverted and thinking framework. Jung saw these years as the most profound turning point in his career, upon which his later theoretical concerns were entirely built.

Jung was aware of the relativity of psychic health and pathology. Normality tells us little about the integration and harmony of the psyche. A normal person may be well-adapted to a sick society. About the so-called normal man in society, the undifferentiated man, Jung said:

> The man of today, who resembles more or less the collective ideal, has made his heart into a den of murderers, as can easily be proved by the analysis of his unconscious, even though he himself is not in the least disturbed by it. And in so far as he is normally "adapted" to his environment, it is true that the greatest infamy on the part of his group will not disturb him, so long as the majority of his fellows steadfastly believe in the exalted morality of their social organization.[42]

Jung's concept of health is not defined by cultural adjustment. How is one to become unpathological in a pathological society? The issue is at the very least a moral one, but the practical considerations of the individual process in their overwhelming difficulty are worthy of consideration. Jung saw that the pathology of society exercises a staggering collective force against the individual. Large communities dominated by conservative prejudices rule heavily against the individual difference. Society's one source of moral and spiritual advancement through the vision of the individual is repeatedly repressed and ignored. Individual elements in the personality from childhood are driven underground, where on the unconscious level they are "transformed into something essentially baseful, destructive, and anarchical. Socially, this evil principle shows itself in the spectacular crimes."[43] Rather than difference and uniqueness, society stresses the mediocrity of collective man. "Individuality will inevitably be driven to the wall. . . . Without freedom there can be no morality."[44]

Jung's life in Switzerland, experiencing two world wars and in particular the Nazi domination, grimly underlined the stark view of the individual, powerless against collective force. When a person enters into an individuation process, there are innumerable collective factors to differentiate from oneself:

There is no doubt, for instance, that archaic symbolisms such as we frequently find in fantasies and dreams are collective factors. All basic instincts and basic forms of thinking and feeling are collective. Everything that all men agree in regarding as universal is collective, likewise everything that is universally understood, universally found, universally said and done. On closer examination one is always astonished to see how much of our so-called individual psychology is really collective. . . . To find out what is truly individual in ourselves, profound reflection is needed; and suddenly we realize how uncommonly difficult the discovery of individuality is.[45]

To differentiate ourselves from collective factors is not to reject them in ourselves or reject the collective aspects of society, but rather to acknowledge their independent existence and not identify them as our possessions or confuse them with our individual expression. In this manner, one does not hold oneself apart from the world so much as exercise an increasing neutrality and choice. Ironically, a normal person developing neurotic symptoms may in fact have taken a step toward his or her own psychic health. Neurosis can be a sign of lifting above. While Jung saw no unified plan on the part of the unconscious to strive toward certain, definite goals, he did recognize an "urge towards self-realization":

There are vast masses of the population who, despite their notorious unconsciousness, never get anywhere near a neurosis. The few who are smitten by such a fate are really persons of the "higher" type who, for one reason or another, have remained too long on a primitive level. Their nature does not in the long run tolerate persistence in what is for them an unnatural torpor. As a result of their narrow conscious outlook and their cramped existence they save energy: bit by bit it accumulates in the unconscious and finally explodes in the form of a more or less acute neurosis. This simple mechanism does not necessarily conceal a "plan." A perfectly understandable urge towards self-realization would provide quite a satisfactory explanation.[46]

The most powerful aspect of Jung was that he came to trust the inside of man, the world of spontaneous images. He stepped through the looking glass. From the position of extroverted science, the inner world was untrustworthy and dangerous. The inner world was to be controlled—understood only to be rendered harmless or exploited. Jung was led to turn inside out, to trust to the intelligence of dreams, to dialogue with people in fantasies, to respect and record spontaneous symbols that wash ashore on the small island of consciousness. He knew that the inner images are the true directors of the outer world.

I think of the Chinese master-artist who painted a landscape and then, in amazing detail, a tiny door in a hillside. At the right moment, he opened the door and disappeared inside. To step inside is to enter the garden of the world, a collective unconscious that we all share in common. It is this garden that we return to, not as an escape but as a way of establishing contact with the determining images of our lives. On the inner levels, the true course and meaning of our lives can be seen, and this understanding must be brought back and grounded in the outer worlds. Dreams are not the only tools available for contact with the underlying images, but they remain the most prolific and immediate.

Notes

1. C. G. Jung, *Modern Man in Search of a Soul*, trans. W. S. Dell and Cary F. Baynes (New York: Harvest, 1933), p. 117.

2. C. G. Jung, *The Psychogenesis of Mental Disease*, trans. R. F. C. Hull, Bollingen Series XX, vol. 3 (Princeton: Princeton University Press, 1960), p. 55.

3. Jung, *Modern Man*, p. 192.

4. Jung, *Psychogenesis*, p. 22.

5. Ibid., p. 28.

6. Ibid., p. 26.

7. Ibid., p. 19.

8. Ibid., p. 40.

9. Ibid., p. 47.

10. C. G. Jung, "The Psychology of Dementia Praecox," in Jung, *Psychogenesis*.

11. C. G. Jung, "Letter of February 5, 1934," in *C. G. Jung Letters*, trans. R. F. C. Hull, ed. Gerhard Adler and Aniela Jaffé, Bollingen Series XCV, vol. 1 (1906–1950) (Princeton: Princeton University Press, 1973), p. 143.

12. Jung, *Psychogenesis*, pp. 261–262.

13. C. G. Jung, *Symbols of Transformation: An Analysis of the Prelude to a Case of Schizophrenia*, 2nd ed., trans. R. F. C. Hull, Bollingen Series XX, vol. 5 (Princeton: Princeton University Press, 1956), p. 101.

14. C. G. Jung, *The Structure and Dynamics of the Psyche*, 2nd ed., trans. R. F. C. Hull, Bollingen Series XX, vol. 8 (Princeton: Princeton University Press, 1969), p. 150.

15. See C. G. Jung, *Memories, Dreams, Reflections*, revised edition, trans. Richard and Clara Winston, ed. Aniela Jaffé (New York: Pantheon, 1973), p. 171.

16. C. G. Jung, *Two Essays on Analytical Psychology*, 2nd ed., trans. R. F. C. Hull, Bollingen Series XX, vol. 7 (Princeton: Princeton University Press, 1972), p. 281.

17. Jung, *Modern Man*, p. 220.

18. Revised edition, trans. Richard and Clara Winston, ed. Aniela Jaffé (New York: Pantheon, 1973).

19. Aldo Carotenuto, *A Secret Symmetry: Sabina Spielrein Between Jung and Freud*, trans. Arno Pomerans, John Shepley, and Krishna Winston (New York: Pantheon, 1982), p. 12, quotes from Sabina's diary entry of September 11, 1910: "His wife is protected by the law, respected by all, and I, who wanted to give him everything I possessed, without the slightest regard for myself, I am called immoral in the language of society—lover, maybe *maîtresse!*"

20. William McGuire, ed., *The Freud/Jung Letters: The Correspondence Between Sigmund Freud and C. G. Jung*, trans. Ralph Manheim and R. F. C. Hull, Bollingen Series XCIV (Princeton: Princeton University Press, 1974), Letter no. 144, June 4, 1909, p. 228.

21. Ibid., p. 236.

22. Bruno Bettelheim, "Scandal in the Family," *New York Review of Books*, 30 (June 30, 1983): 39.

23. At a Transpersonal Conference that I attended in 1983 in Davos, Switzerland, Marie-Louise von Franz, longtime friend and working companion of Jung, was asked about Bettelheim's assumption that Jung slept with Sabina Spielrein. Von Franz replied that she knew all about their relationship and that they did not have an affair.

24. McGuire, ed., *Freud/Jung Letters*, Letter no. 98j, June 19, 1908, p. 155.

25. Ibid., Letter no. 144, June 4, 1909, p. 229.

26. Ibid., Letter no. 247j, March 31, 1911, p. 412.

27. François Roustang, *Dire Mastery: Discipleship from Freud to Lacan*, trans. Ned Lukacher (Baltimore: Johns Hopkins University Press, 1982), pp. 88–89.

28. Ibid., p. 39.

29. Ibid., p. 44.

30. Ibid., p. 53.

31. Jung, *Symbols of Transformation*, pp. 418–419.

32. Ibid., p. 420.

33. Ibid.

34. Lou Andreas-Salomé, *The Freud Journal of Lou Andreas-Salomé*, trans. Stanley A. Leavy (New York: Basic Books, 1964), p. 43.

35. Ibid., pp. 168–169.

36. Jung, *Memories, Dreams, Reflections*, pp. 170–171.

37. Ibid., p. 170.

38. C. G. Jung, *Psychological Types*, trans. H. G. Baynes, ed. R. F. C. Hull, Bollingen Series XX, vol. 6 (Princeton: Princeton University Press, 1976), p. 330.

39. Barbara Hannah, *Jung: His Life and Work—A Biographical Memoir* (New York: Putnam's, 1976), p. 116.

40. Ibid., pp. 115–116.

41. Jung, *Memories, Dreams, Reflections*, p. 183.

42. Jung, *Two Essays*, p. 154.

43. Ibid., p. 153.

44. Ibid.

45. Ibid., p. 155.

46. Ibid., p. 184.

Chapter 6

The Shadow

I stood upon a high place
And saw, below, many devils
Running, leaping,
And carousing in sin.
One looked up, grinning,
And said: "Comrade! Brother!"

—Stephen Crane

Jung understood the sickness in Western culture that denies the opposites in human nature. As a child in a minister's family, he was thrust into the heart of a Christianity that denied the dark side, denied the value of doubt. At his first communion, he expectantly waited for the subjective experience of profound change, but felt nothing.

When he was eleven years old, he was tortured by a vision in which he saw God on his throne above the cathedral in Basel. As he saw this remarkable vision, a terrible thought threatened to break through, but he was terrified to let himself think further, lest his thoughts damn him. Finally, after days of anguish, he decided to let his mind express itself, and he saw a huge turd from God's throne fall and destroy the roof and walls of the cathedral. Rather than damnation, he experienced release and a sense of grace.

These feelings enforced Jung's sense of being an outsider. There appeared to be no room in the Christian cultural fabric to include the shadow. His mother suggested that he read Goethe's *Faust*, and that became a guiding myth for his life, a story that did full justice to the integration of the "dark side."

Later, particularly in *The Answer to Job*, Jung expressed the dilemma that Christianity faces by splitting the opposites of light and darkness, masculinity and femininity. Christ is all good, and Christians are expected to see no value in "sin." The devil serves no serious function in life. God is male. The Church is the Bride of Christ, but that hardly brings the feminine into the God-head. For that reason, Jung was gratified at the Roman Catholic doctrine of the Assumption of the Virgin, which squares the trinity precisely by bringing the feminine into the Godhead. In contrast to the dismissive polarizing of good and evil in the developing Christian Church, the Gnostics proclaimed that God includes the opposites, both darkness and light—that God is accountable for *all* of creation. Therefore, darkness is as essential as light in man's evolution, providing the testing ground to develop his inner nature.

The psyche of man as a microcosm of the world likewise contains the opposites of light and dark. What is denied is thrust into unconsciousness and lives its secret within the shadows of one's life. When a culture splits the opposites in man, denies the shadow, and exalts the masculine over the feminine virtues, it dooms itself to wars and unexpected reigns of terror, as the dark side, so long denied a voice, erupts after long suppression. Reich saw evil as a secondary layer originating from the perversion of free and full expression of the sexual instinct, but Jung saw evil in a more global way.

In the individuation process, it is necessary to accept the opposites, to expect the good man to have moments of rage, to include the dark lessons of life that lead us to the holy grail. The way toward God could be toward an uplifted consciousness, a deepened awareness rather than an adherence to "good" behavior. Man's fall from Eden was his first step in awakening, and the awakening of man was his salvation. Submission and obedience do not bring enlightenment. To begin instead to see life as most powerfully alive in its opposites is to live vitally, intelligently, and cooperatively with one's spiritual path.

Each of us has a shadow side and a masculine or feminine counterpart within us, animus or anima, created in the natural thrust of the law of opposites. The integration of the shadow and the bisexual nature of the psyche is essential in the path of individuation.

Jung drew from language rich with connotations. The shadow as concept and experience is pervasive in life and art. Abundant and common as salt, yet it remains as changeable, elusive, and lethal as the power of imagination itself. Everything on the planet that feels the light must cast a fragile dark shape, which in fact confirms to the eye that an object has bulk, has three dimensions.

Jung differentiated between the personal shadow, the collective shadow, and the archetypal shadow. As Marie-Louise von Franz has said:

> In Jungian psychology, we generally define the shadow as the personification of certain aspects of the unconscious personality, which could be added to the ego complex but which, for various reasons, are not. We might therefore say that the shadow is the dark, unlived, and repressed side of the ego complex, but this is only partly true.[1]

Jung tended to pull away from definitions of his terminology when they were too rigidly applied. Again, to quote von Franz:

> Dr. Jung, who hates it when his pupils are too literal minded and cling to his concepts and make a system out of them and quote him without knowing exactly what they are saying, once in a discussion threw all this over and said, "This is all nonsense! The shadow is simply the whole unconscious."[2]

Consciousness is just a focus of light moving in the darkness, and in the shadows stand not just what we dare not see but our potentiality, what we are becoming. In Jung's words:

> That future personality which we are to be in a year's time is already here, only it is still in the shadow. The ego is like a moving frame on a film. The future personality is not yet visible, but we are moving along, and presently we come to view the future being. These potentialities naturally belong to the dark side of the ego.[3]

While our tendency is to turn from the darkness in fear and to see there only what we assume is inferior and unworthy, psychology teaches us to enter more easily into the shadows so that we can cooperate with nature and ourselves. As Jung wrote:

> Consciousness, no matter how extensive it may be, must always remain the smaller circle within the greater circle of the unconscious, an island surrounded by the sea; and, like the sea itself, the unconscious yields an endless and self-replenishing abundance of living creatures, a wealth beyond our fathoming. We may long have known the meaning, effects, and characteristics of unconscious contents without ever having fathomed their depths and potentialities, for they are capable of infinite variation and can never be depotentiated. The only way to get at them in practice is to try to attain a conscious attitude which allows the unconscious to cooperate instead of being driven into opposition.[4]

The hero's journey leads into the unconscious, the shadow of present social being. John Bunyan, in *The Pilgrim's Progress*, begins with a step into unconsciousness, experiencing as he does so a sense of alienation: "As I walked through the wilderness of this world," he says, "I lighted on a certain place, where was a den; and as I slept I dreamed a dream."[5] And Dante also goes astray in a midlife crisis:

> Midway in our life's journey, I went astray
> from the straight road and woke to find myself
> alone in a dark wood, How shall I say
>
> what wood that was! I never saw so drear,
> so rank, so arduous a wilderness!
> Its very memory gives a shape to fear.[6]

Thus, we can see something of the range of the concept, extending from the personal shadow into the entire shadow that surrounds the small candlelight of our consciousness. The shadow on a personal level may contain not only the discarded and rejected aspects of ourselves but the potentiality of being. As Goethe said, "Coming events cast their shadow before."[7]

The shadow is what gives us three dimensions, grounds us in the present reality, demonstrates our presence on the physical plane, and demonstrates our membership among those who are subject to the pain and constriction of time. The shadow holds the essence of what it is to be alive.

The spirit world does not cast a shadow, is not grounded here; it is neither responsible to the laws of this world nor able to grasp its strange privileges. The shadow gives us weight and credibility, grounds us in space and time. The physical world, with its trying limitations, holds a fascination for the ungrounded spirit world. "Eternity," said William Blake, "is in love with the productions of time."[8] The gods are not content to stay on Olympus. They consort with humankind.

Life is played out through a tension of opposites. The light is often seen as reason, order, that which conforms, stands forward, looks good, relates easily to other parts, is scientific, empirical, predictable, understood, generally agreed on, immediately available, civilized, in balance, the right hand, structure, sanity, the face of things, the Apollonian, the leaves, branches, and trunk of the tree.

The shadow, in contrast, is imagined, unseen, primitive, archaic, instinctual, primordial, unpredictable, confused, rebellious, unstructured, unaccepted, unrelated, uncivilized, unstable, unavailable, mad, the left hand, the antithetical mask, the Dionysian, the underside of things, the chthonic side, the background, the peripheral, the perverse, the yearned for, that which holds back and stands back, that which is glimpsed at out of the corner of the eye, that which looks bad, is magical, denied, unusual, mercurial, elusive, deadly, underground, the roots of the tree.

On the one hand, said Jung, "sinful, empirical man" stands opposed to "Primordial Man," the primitive man, a "shadow of our present-day consciousness," who "has his roots in the animal man (the tailed Adam), who has long since vanished from our consciousness. Even the primitive man has become a stranger to us, so that we have to rediscover his psychology. It was therefore something of a surprise when analytical psychology discovered in the products of the unconscious of modern man so much archaic material—and not only that, but the sinister darkness of the animal world of instinct."[9] The instinctual and primitive, all that falls on the dark side, is for the most part avoided by society.

Jung also said that "the man without a shadow is statistically the commonest human type, one who imagines he actually is only what he cares to know about himself."[10] In families, for instance, the children or other family members may act out the shadow that has been denied by another family member. Frequently the children in families act out the unconscious yearnings of the parents, which play vibrantly, albeit unconsciously, throughout their childhood. A. I. Allensby, a Jungian analyst in England, recalls a story told to him by Jung:

> He told me that he once met a distinguished man, a Quaker, who could not imagine that he had ever done anything wrong in his life. "And do you know what happened to his children?" Jung asked. "The son became a thief, and the daughter a prostitute. Because the father would not take on his shadow, his share in the imperfection of human nature, his children were compelled to live out the dark side which he had ignored.[11]

To remain a man without a shadow is to live as a mass man, projecting onto others the wrongs of the world, supported by a shallow righteousness, easily subject to the collective forces of life. Without his shadow, modern man has no ground, no individual sense of meaning. "Modern man," Jung argued, "must rediscover a deeper source of his own spiritual life. To do this, he is obliged to struggle with evil, to confront his shadow, to integrate the devil. There is no other choice."[12] The aim is a synthesis of opposites, the assimilation of the darkness, an acceptance and rejuvenation through the acknowledgment of the more primitive instinctual side, the inferior side. But the personal shadow, Jung concluded, is linked with a darkness that will never be completely assimilated:

> In psychological terms, the soul finds itself in the throes of melancholy, locked in a struggle with the "shadow." The mystery of the *coniunction*, the central mystery of alchemy, aims precisely at the synthesis of opposites, the assimilation of the blackness, the integration of the devil. For the "awakened" Christian this is a very serious psychic experience, for it is a confrontation with his own "shadow," with the blackness, the nigredo, which remains separate and can never be completely integrated into the human personality.[13]

Perhaps most powerfully on a personal level, the shadow becomes a sparring partner, the opponent who sharpens our skill.

The shadow comes to us in the form of a thorn in the side, a person or event that appears to block our expansion, interrupt our joy, and negate our plans. The shadow comes to us in the area of our greatest blindness, an area of inferior development where we are least able to defend ourselves, an area where we are least subtle and least differentiated. Jung wrote about this:

> I should only like to point out that the inferior function is practically identical with the dark side of the human personality. The darkness which clings to every personality is the door into the unconscious and the gateway of dreams, from which those two twilight figures, the shadow and the anima, step into our nightly visions or, remaining invisible, take possession of our ego-consciousness. A man who is possessed by his shadow is always standing in his own light and falling into his own traps.[14]

Coming as it does to that part of us where we feel least defended, our shadow makes us act explosively and catastrophically, and, inevitably, we wish to be rid of it. Thomas à Becket was such a shadow figure for Henry the Second. Whatever person or situation we project the shadow upon becomes our devil, the enemy, and at best the beloved enemy. Since a shadow figure often stands on our blind side, it can see us as we would prefer not to see ourselves, and we become uneasy. The beloved enemy stands at the door of our unconscious. It comments loudly to us and points out our repeated failing, our lack of skill in an area we are ill-equipped to develop. Such events or persons need to be embraced without our trying to win them over.

Often the crudest shadow figures are there as our teachers. In our resistance and denial, we are unable to hear the kinder, more indirect language of our friends, or we force them into silence with our sensitivity or ruthless denial. But one comes to us who is unswayed by our fragility or manipulation. He (or she) is the beloved enemy, a shadow aspect standing before us, apparently blocking our way. Frequently his rough-hewn attitude and manner perfectly describe an inner aspect of our own willful stubbornness. In this way, the shadow may in fact be our best teacher, reflecting back to us our blind side.

The great danger of ridding ourselves of a shadow figure is described in the New Testament (Matthew 12:43–45), where a man drives out one devil that possesses him, but that devil goes and tells seven others of the vacancy, and they return to occupy him once more.

The least developed part of our personality, the side opposite our major gifts and strengths, is the area known in Jungian terms as the fourth function. It is in this area that the shadow stands to educate us and provoke our outrage, shock, and resistance. As this fourth function is developed and faced, the entire structure of the personality gains breadth and stability and loses its one-sided self-righteousness, shifting from rigidity to flexibility.

To some degree, a therapist must stand on our shadow side in such a way that we grow familiar with and used to an alien presence who stands on our blind side without judgment. The transformer, the agent of change, must be able to pass through the borders from light into the land of darkness and be equally at home. He must be one who is well acquainted with the wilderness and the desert, with the dark, left-handed ways. Mythically he has been represented by Hermes (Mercury), the messenger of the gods, the protector of thieves and god of the borders, appearing often in the bodily form of early adolescence, in which the masculine and feminine aspects are gently blended. But, of course, if the shadow terrifies us, he will take on more the form of the devil, the one who tests and opposes us, and even seeks our destruction. "Opposition," said William Blake, "is true friendship."[15]

Not only do individuals create shadows, but so do groups, organizations, and nations. As we develop and project an ego ideal on the one hand, gradually a shadow form develops on the other. The United States, with its ideals of liberty and justice, has also in the shadows the death of the Indian and the enslavement of the black man. The most obvious example of the collective shadow is provided by Nazi Germany. Hitler, Jung saw in 1938, was the "medicine man," the "loudspeaker which magnifies the inaudible whispers of the German soul."[16] "As soon as people get together in masses and submerge the individual, the shadow is mobilized, and, as history shows, may even be personified and incarnated."[17]

> Like the rest of the world, they [the German people] did not understand wherein Hitler's significance lay, that he symbolized something in every individual. He was the most prodigious

personification of all human inferiorities. He was an utterly incapable, unadapted, irresponsible, psychopathic personality, full of empty, infantile fantasies, but cursed with the keen intuition of a rat or a guttersnipe. He represented the shadow, the inferior part of everybody's personality, in an overwhelming degree, and this was another reason why they fell for him.

But what could they have done? In Hitler, every German should have seen his own shadow, his own worst danger. It is everybody's allotted fate to become conscious of and learn to deal with this shadow. But how could the Germans be expected to understand this, when nobody in the world can understand such a simple truth?[18]

One would have to acknowledge that the meeting with the collective shadow is sufficiently terrifying. We prefer to deal with these issues historically or as projections. There is always the sense that evil can be identified by reason and engaged in with meaning, or psychically avoided. Beyond the personal projections lies the archetypal shadow itself, always present, ready to be reunited, sitting intimately among us as one of our most loyal friends. "But, behold," said Jesus, "the hand of him that betrayeth me is with me on the table" (Luke 22:21). To suddenly slip past the humanity we expect and stare into the eyes of something "inhuman" is to catch a glimpse of the archetypal shadow. "In other words," wrote Jung, "it is quite within the bounds of possibility for a man to recognize the relative evil of his nature, but it is a rare and shattering experience for him to gaze into the face of absolute evil."[19]

Trevor Ravenscroft believes that the "innermost circle of Nazidom were self-confessed satanists,"[20] that supporting Hitler were adepts in the black arts, Eckart, Haushofer, and Heilscher, and that the "Luciferic Principality inhabiting the soul of Hitler sought by means of racist doctrines to lead mankind away from an inward recognition of the Individual Human Spirit."[21] Ravenscroft's documented argument brings the sense of the archetypal shadow a little closer to home.

A sinister description of the Doppelgänger (double) appears in Ravenscroft's *The Spear of Destiny*. "There exists in every human being," he writes, "a kind of 'anti-man' . . . which occultism calls the 'Double.'"[22] Goethe spoke of a time when, entering his study in

Weimar, he saw what appeared to be himself, a counterpart sitting in his chair "behind his desk and looking brazenly back at him." For a few seconds he was able to stare into the eyes and leering face of his counterpart. "It was the first of several such experiences through which the poet came to understand the reason for the existence of this merciless and inhuman shadow element in the human soul."[23] The purpose of the shadow is to provide the human soul with the opposition and tension to develop tough inner resolve and determination, to clarify through the challenge of opposites and awaken us so that we are available for profound transformation.

Notes

1. Marie-Louise von Franz, *Shadow and Evil in Fairytales* (Zurich: Spring Publications, 1974), p. 5.

2. Ibid.

3. C. G. Jung, *Analytical Psychology: Its Theory and Practice* (New York: Vintage, 1968), p. 22.

4. C. G. Jung, *The Practice of Psychotherapy: Essays on the Psychology of the Transference and Other Subjects*, 2nd ed., trans. R. F. C. Hull, Bollingen Series XX, vol. 16 (Princeton: Princeton University Press, 1966), p. 14.

5. John Bunyan, *The Pilgrim's Progress*, ed. Roger Shamrock (Harmondsworth, England: Penguin, 1965), p. 39.

6. Dante Alighieri, *The Inferno*, trans. John Ciardi (New York: Mentor, 1954), p. 28.

7. Quoted here from Trevor Ravenscroft, *The Spear of Destiny* (New York: Putnam's, 1973), p. 21.

8. William Blake, "Proverbs of Hell," in *Poems and Letters*, ed. J. Bronowski (Middlesex, England: Penguin, 1986), p. 96.

9. C. G. Jung, *Mysterium Coniunctionis: An Inquiry into the Separation and Synthesis of Psychic Opposites in Alchemy*, 2nd ed., trans. R. F. C. Hull, Bollingen Series XX, vol. 14 (Princeton: Princeton University Press, 1977), p. 417.

10. C. G. Jung, *The Structure and Dynamics of the Psyche*, 2nd ed., trans. R. F. C. Hull, Bollingen Series XX, vol. 8 (Princeton: Princeton University Press, 1969), p. 208.

11. William McGuire and R. F. C. Hull, eds., *C. G. Jung Speaking: Interviews and Encounters*, Bollingen Series XVII (Princeton: Princeton University Press, 1972), p. 158.

12. Ibid., p. 230.

13. Ibid., p. 228.

14. C. G. Jung, *The Archetypes and the Collective Unconscious*, trans. R. F. C. Hull, ed. Sir Herbert Read, Michael Fordham, and Gerhard Adler, Bollingen Series XX, vol. 9 (Princeton: Princeton University Press, 1980), p. 123.

15. Blake, *Poems and Letters*, p. 105.

16. McGuire and Hull, eds., *Jung Speaking*, p. 118.

17. C. G. Jung, *Four Archetypes: Mother/Rebirth/Spirit/Trickster*, trans. R. F. C. Hull, Bollingen Series XX, vol. 9 (Princeton: Princeton University Press, 1970), p. 147.

18. C. G. Jung, *Civilization in Transition*, 2nd ed., trans. R. F. C. Hull, Bollingen Series XX, vol. 10 (Princeton: Princeton University Press, 1970), p. 223.

19. C. G. Jung, *AION: Researches into the Phenomenology of the Self*, 2nd ed., trans. R. F. C. Hull, Bollingen Series XX, vol. 9 (Princeton: Princeton University Press, 1968), p. 10.

20. Ravenscroft, *Spear*, p. 261.

21. Ibid., p. 262.

22. Ibid., p. 290.

23. Ibid., p. 129.

Chapter 7

The Double as the Immortal Self

Who, if I shouted, among the hierarchy of angels
Would hear me? And supposing one of them
took me suddenly to his heart, I would perish
before his stronger existence. For beauty is nothing
but the beginning of terror we can just barely endure,
and we admire it so because it calmly disdains
to destroy us. Every angel is terrible.
And so I restrain myself and swallow the living call
of dark sobbing. Oh, whom can we use then?
Not angels, not men, and the shrewd animals
notice that we're not very much at home
in the world we've expounded. Maybe on the hill-slope
some tree or other remains for us, so that
we see it every day; yesterday's street is left us,
and the guarded fidelity of an old habit
that was comfortable with us and never wanted to leave.

—Rainer Maria Rilke, *The Duino Elegies*

Throughout his brilliant career, Otto Rank was drawn to the concept of the double. Introduced to Freud in 1905, at the age of twenty-two, by his physician, Alfred Adler, he was soon adopted into Freud's circle, becoming secretary, lay analyst, editor of the official psychoanalytical publication, and favorite son until 1924. The intimacy between Freud and Rank seems unparalleled, so that his breaking away from Freud after years of collaboration and support is a bitter story and largely unexplained. Paul Roazen, in *Freud and His Followers*, suggests that Freud's brush with death from cancer of the jaw in 1923 triggered the separation unconsciously for both of them, but was assisted by the jealousy of Freud's other followers, particularly Karl Abraham and Ernest Jones.[1]

But Rank, with his breadth of learning in literature, his fascination with mythology, and eventually his defection from the mechanistic science of psychoanalysis, had a great deal in common with Jung, although he would hardly have admitted it. After years of seeing Jung and Adler as defectors, he was not likely to turn suddenly and recognize a brother. In his last book, *Beyond Psychology*, Rank lumped Jung, Adler, and Freud together in a way that did Jung little justice, describing him as creating "more nearly a subjective psychology of the individual than do either Freud or Adler."[2] Rather than calling Jung's concept of the collective unconscious by that name, Rank used a more pejorative term, "racial unconscious":

> In this psychological process of sublimation, the individual, according to Jung, makes use of the symbolism in his racial unconscious, thus achieving as it were a kind of collectivity within his own self. Such a striving towards an almost mystical union between the self and its racial background is supposed to link the isolated individual with a bigger whole of which he can feel an essential part. . . . In their different attempts to work out a psychology of the individual, all three seem to have reached a similar conclusion, namely, that the evil from which our personality suffers is over-individualization; hence, they agree in the remedy consisting of an emotional unity with something beyond the Self. Freud sees it in sex, Adler in social fellowship, and Jung in racial collectivity. In this sense, psychology is searching for a substitute for the cosmic unity which the man of Antiquity enjoyed in life and expressed in his religion, but which modern man has lost—a loss which accounts for the developing of the neurotic type.[3]

Much of the later Rank is in harmony with Jungian thought. Rank had first published a study of the double in 1914,[4] and then a more complete one in 1925.[5] Finally, his concepts were developed further in a chapter in *Beyond Psychology*, where scientific agnosticism shifts to a gentler awareness and acceptance of human nature. In 1925, he wrote that the belief in immortality is merely an energetic denial of death:

> In this way, therefore, the primitive belief in souls is originally nothing else than a kind of belief in immortality which energetically denies the power of death; and even today the essential content of the belief in the soul—as it subsists in religion, superstition, and modern cults—has not become other, nor much more, than that. The thought of death is rendered supportable by assuring oneself of a second life, after this one, as a double.[6]

By 1939, Rank was writing: "Psychology, in other words, is not an objective instrument, like a telescope or microscope; . . . it is not a science beyond or about the civilization it presumes to explain"— a viewpoint identical to Jung's.[7] In "The Double as Immortal Self," Rank's attitudes about spiritual matters had matured. "Civilized man," he wrote, "does not act only upon the rational guidance of his intellectual ego, nor is he driven blindly by the mere elemental forces of his instinctual self," but he has emerged because of a third principle, "which combines the rational and irrational elements in a world-view based on the conception of the supernatural."[8] This view was not only valuable to primitive group life but "is still borne out in our highly mechanized civilization by the vital need for spiritual values."[9]

> That is to say, what we really have in common with our remote ancestors is a *spiritual*, not a primitive self, and this we cannot afford to admit because we pride ourselves on living on a purely rational plane. In consequence, we reject those irrational life forces as belonging to our primitive past instead of recognizing them in our present spiritual needs.[10]

The basis for culture, said Rank, is man's supernatural worldview, from which springs drama, architecture, and the other arts. "Man creates culture by changing natural conditions in order to maintain his spiritual self."[11] Within man stands his "still living ancestor, the spiritual self or primitive man."[12] The over-civilized ego of modern man "disintegrates by splitting up the latter into two opposing selves."[13]

Rank saw modern psychology as trying to render rational what is and will remain irrational in human nature, and, inaccurately, he accused Jung of reducing the unconscious through rational means:

> Thus while all three psychologists admitted the extra-individual quality of the unconscious, they all rationalized it in terms of their respective individual psychology, thereby missing its real meaning, namely, that this increasingly denied side of human nature always was and will be potent—and if frustrated breaks through in neurotic or anti-social, i.e., irrational behavior.[14]

Rank also slurred Jung's character, as did others, by mistakenly considering him a Nazi sympathizer and an anti-Semite. In 1933, Jung's brief engagement with the Nazi hierarchy in his role as president of the International General Medical Society for Psychotherapy and editor of its publication *Zentralblatt* was an attempt to save the society from Hitler's destruction by reorganizing it and by publishing a special issue of the journal, to be distributed only in Germany, to pacify the German authorities. This awkward but well-intentioned effort to protect the analysts he knew in Germany became indispensable to Jung's enemies, who had no investment in understanding his thoughts or motives. Many of the same psychoanalysts who criticized Jung thought nothing of driving the Marxist Wilhelm Reich from their midst in 1933, lest Hitler take offense. It was a time of terror and confusion.

Rank succumbed to the pattern of all of Freud's rebellious children, who would have been better off if they had talked to one another. Rank and Jung shared a fascination with primitive man and the study of myth, an awareness of the central importance of the spiritual archetype in man, disillusionment with the concept of objective science in the field of psychology, and the concept of neurosis in modern man. Rank's outstanding work on the double as seen in primitive tribes, folklore, and modern literature adds enormous richness to the concept of the shadow. The double includes the shadow, man's reflection in mirrors and water, identical twins, and other intense relationships in which two people are seen as aspects of a whole. While the double as a term is inclusive, I prefer to use it in the restricted context of the immortal self.

Rank felt that the representation of a second self by one's own shadow or reflection may have been man's first conception of the soul:

Numerous superstitions regarding one's shadow or image still prevalent in all parts of our civilized world correspond to widespread tabus of primitives who see in this natural image of the self the human soul. . . . Primitive people are not only afraid to let their shadow fall on certain objects, especially food, but also dread the accidental falling upon them of the shadows of other people— above all, those of pregnant women and mothers-in-law. They are careful that no person shall ever cross their shadow and take special care that their shadows do not fall on the dead, or on the coffin, or a tomb—one reason, it is supposed, why their burials often take place at night. Their greatest fear, however, concerns the intentional injury of their shadow by means of magic, since according to a common belief an enemy can be killed by the wounding of his shadow. Many other folk traditions of a similar kind clearly indicate that primitive man considers the shadow his mysterious double, a spiritual yet real being.[15]

Rank saw that the origin of religion was the belief in the soul of the dead, and that psychology eventually developed from the belief in the soul present in the living. He postulated that man first associated his immortal soul with the shadow by observing the latter's death and reappearance with the daily cycle of the sun. From the work of a classical scholar, Erwin Rohde, Rank extracted an interesting quotation concerning man's dual nature as understood by Homer:

According to Homer, man has a dualistic existence, the one in his visible appearance, the other in his invisible image which becomes free only after death— this, and no other, is his soul. In animate man there dwells as a strange guest a more feeble Double—his other Self in the form of his Psyche—whose kingdom is the world of dreams. When the conscious Self sleeps, the Double works and watches. Such an image (*eidolon*) reflecting the visible Self and constituting a second Self is, with the Romans, the Genius; with the Persians, the Fravauli; with the Egyptians, the Ka.[16]

The double, according to Rank, shifts from an assurance of the immortal self to an omen of death. The Christian doctrine and churches, which presumed to judge good and bad souls, established "the cult of the Devil, who in essence is nothing but a personification of the moralized double."[17] In Goethe's *Faust*, the struggle with the devil becomes the search for self-realization. In modern literature, the double frequently represents the tortured split in the personality of the writer. In the case of Dostoievski, for instance:

> According to Merejkovsky, the theme of the Double was for Dostoievski his main personal problem; "Thus all his tragic and struggling pairs of real people who appear to themselves as complete entities are presented as two halves of a third divided personality—halves which, like the doubles, seek themselves and pursue themselves." This is carried out in the most grandiose manner in his last and greatest novel, *The Brothers Karamazov*, where Smerjakov is pictured as the double of his brother Ivan, the two not only usually appearing together and discussing the same subjects, but being inseparably united by a favorite motif of Dostoievski's, the idea of the potential criminal. This double (says Ivan) "is only a personification of myself, in fact only a part of myself . . . of my lowest and stupidest thoughts and feelings."[18]

In the use of the double to represent the criminal, low, stupid side of ourselves, we have a concept that is in keeping with Jung's concept of the personal shadow, the repressed and despised aspect, the dark side of the ego. In Robert Louis Stevenson's *Dr. Jeckyl and Mr. Hyde*, Hyde is a shadow figure, just as the ever-changing picture of Dorian Gray is the shadow for the ageless adolescent beauty.

Rank tells of an actual experience in 1889 of Guy de Maupassant, who was seated at his desk in his study, having given strict orders that no one was to be admitted:

> Suddenly he had the impression that someone had opened the door. He turned around and to his great astonishment saw his own self enter and sit down in front of him, resting his head on his hand. All that Maupassant wrote on this occasion was dictated to him by his double. Having finished, he rose and the phantom vanished.[19]

But the double as the immortal self stands separate from the concept of the shadow and may appear in life and in dreams as a figure, a double who challenges us; a more vital, perhaps more primitive self, but hardly the shadow side of the ego. Jung was apparently aware of the concept of the double. In a seminar he conducted in 1936–37, he commented on the appearance of a magic mirror in a child's dream, and on the dark side of the double:

> Among the ancient Greeks also, when the mirror appeared in a dream, it was considered uncanny. It indicated the death of the person, because the picture that one saw in the mirror was one's own double. It is the Ka of the Egyptians. It is a soul-image. That is why the primitives don't want to be photographed, for fear that their double, their soul-image, would be taken away, and that a loss of soul would ensue.
>
> When one sees one's double, it indicates death. Narcissus sees his image and drowns in it. The student of Prague who sells his own image to the devil is no longer with an image, which means: the soul has gone from the body and that signifies misfortune. We find the same problem in Chamisso in "Peter Schlemihl," who has no shadow, and in Oscar Wilde's "The Picture of Dorian Gray."[20]

In a paper entitled "The Double: An Archetypal Configuration," Mitchell Walker also sees the value of the concept of the double: "I would like to propose an archetypal concept, the 'double,' to cover a soul figure with all the erotic and spiritual significances attached to anima/us, but of the same sex, and yet not a shadow. This figure has mythological examples, and is felt in psychological experience. It is lost if named either shadow or anima/us."[21] The double is revealed in such hero pairs as David and Jonathan, Achilles and Patroklos, and Gilgamesh and Enkidu, and is characterized by physical beauty, youth, and heroic accomplishment:

> As these myths suggest, the double is a soul-mate of intense warmth and closeness. Love between men and love between women, as a psychic experience, is often rooted in projection of the double, just as anima/us is projected in love between the different sexes. And as with anima/us, such love may occur within or without the heroic quest. Furthermore, since the double is a soul figure, the sexual instinct may or may not become involved. That is, the double motif may include a tendency to homosexuality, but is not necessarily a homosexual archetype. Rather the double embodies the spirit of love between those of the same sex. And the spirit of love in the double is what I see as the supportive ground of the ego.[22]

Traveling in North Africa in 1920 with friends, Jung was strongly impressed by a proud, elegant Arab who rode by without noticing them—Europeans with their pocket watches and their uneasy sense of time. Soon thereafter, Jung had a dream in which he was in an Arab city situated on a plain and surrounded by a square wall with four gates and a moat over which extended a wooden bridge. To challenge his entrance, there appeared a figure hard to characterize, a double with aspects of shadow to him. Jung decided that he was not a personal shadow figure but "a kind of shadow of the self,"[23] a somewhat unexplored category:

> Eager to see the citadel from the inside also, I stepped out on the bridge. When I was about halfway across it, a handsome, dark Arab of aristocratic, almost royal bearing came toward me from the gate. I knew that this youth in the white burnoose was the resident prince of the citadel. When he came up to me, he attacked me and tried to knock me down. We wrestled.[24]

This figure who appears to Jung is larger than the more typical Jungian categories. Like Jacob's angel, he appears in creative opposition, more vital, containing some aspects of an ego-ideal, some seed of our identity; a soul image, a creative potential, a test; most definitely a double archetype.

One place where the archetype of the double is explored without being labeled as such is in Jung's essay "Concerning Rebirth" (1939). Jung describes how, in the individuation process, natural transformations occur, since Nature herself demands a death and a rebirth, and these transformations announce themselves mainly in dreams.[25] One aspect of rebirth symbolism is the transformation into the "other being," "that larger and greater personality maturing within us, whom we have already met as the inner friend of the soul."[26]

> That is why we take comfort whenever we find the friend and companion depicted in a ritual, an example being the friendship between Mithras and the sun god. . . . It is the representation of a friendship between two men which is simply the outer reflection of an inner fact: it reveals our relationship to that inner friend of the soul into whom Nature herself would like to change us—that other person who we also are and yet can never attain to completely. We

are that pair of Dioscuri, one of whom is mortal and the other immortal, and who, though always together, can never be made completely one.[27]

Whether that inner person, so "strange and uncanny," is confronted as a friend or foe depends on us. Sometimes this other presence, known primarily as an inner voice, is treated either as utter madness or as the voice of God. Jung proposes a more moderate third approach whereby one engages in a colloquy with this inner friend. But, he warns, not everyone is up to such a dialogue, for if one is in conversation with Jacob's angel, then the supremacy of the ego is truly shaken and one comes "near to the fire."

> Something of this sort may have been in the mind of the alchemist who wrote: "Choose for your Stone him through whom kings are honored in their crowns, and through whom physicians heal their sick, for he is near to the fire." The alchemists projected the inner event into an outer figure, so for them the inner friend appeared in the form of the "Stone."[28]

Through the work of transformation (individuation), the alchemist turned to Hermes (or Mercurius, in his Roman incarnation). "From the earliest times, Hermes was the mystagogue and psychopomp of the alchemists, their friend and counselor, who leads them to the goal of their work." He is "like a teacher mediating between the son and the disciple." To others, the friend might appear as the Christ or another great spiritual teacher. Through the dialogue with the immortal one within us, we shake off the "mortal Husk," our secondary layer.[29]

> The alchemists saw it in the transformation of the chemical substance. So if one of them sought transformation, he discovered it outside in matter, whose transformation cried out to him, as it were, "I am the transformation!" But some were clever enough to know, "It is my own transformation—not a personal transformation, but the transformation of what is mortal in me into what is immortal. It shakes off the mortal husk that I am and awakens to a life of its own; it mounts the sun-barge and may take me with it."[30]

The Self is personified in the immortal side of the double, before whose power our smaller existence as ego self must not crumble. Unlike the Eastern adept, the Western mystic does not abandon the ego without grave loss. Rather, it is in the sustaining of the smaller self, the trial and chastening of the smaller self, that a new balance is achieved and the individuation process furthered:

> When a summit of life is reached, when the bud unfolds and from the lesser the greater emerges, then, as Nietzsche says, "One becomes Two," and the greater figure, which one always was but which remained invisible, appears to the lesser personality with the force of a revelation. He who is truly and hopelessly little will always drag the revelation of the greater down to the level of his littleness, and will never understand that the day of judgment for his littleness has dawned. But the man who is inwardly great will know that the long-expected friend of his soul, the immortal one, has now really come, "to lead captivity captive."[31]

Notes

1. Paul Roazen, *Freud and His Followers* (New York: Mentor, 1974), pp. 401ff.

2. Otto Rank, *Beyond Psychology* (New York: Dover, 1941), p. 36.

3. Ibid., p. 37.

4. Otto Rank, "Der Doppelgänger," *Imago*, 3 (1914): 97–164.

5. Otto Rank, *Der Doppelgänger: Eine Psychoanalytische Studie* (Leipzig, Vienna, and Zurich: Internationaler Psychoanalytischer Verlag, 1925)—later published as *The Double: A Psychoanalytic Study*, trans. and ed. Harry Tucker, Jr. (New York: Meridian, 1971).

6. Ibid., pp. 84–85.

7. Rank, *Beyond Psychology*, p. 27.

8. Ibid., p. 62.

9. Ibid.

10. Ibid., p. 63.

11. Ibid.. p. 64.

12. Ibid., p. 65.

13. Ibid.

14. Ibid., p. 39.

15. Ibid., p. 71.

16. Ibid., p. 75. The quote is from Erwin Rohde, *Psyche* (Leipzig, 1893).

17. Rank, *Beyond Psychology*, p. 76.

18. Ibid., p. 81.

19. Ibid., p. 79.

20. C. G. Jung, "A Seminar with C. G. Jung: Comments on a Child's Dream (1936–37)," *Spring 1974* (1974): 205–206.

21. Mitchell Walker, "The Double: An Archetypal Configuration," *Spring 1976* (1976): 165.

22. Ibid., p. 169.

23. C. G. Jung, *Memories, Dreams, Reflections*, rev. ed., trans. Richard and Clara Winston, ed. Aniela Jaffé (New York: Pantheon, 1973), p. 245.

24. Ibid., pp. 242–243.

25. C. G. Jung, *The Archetypes and the Collective Unconscious*, trans. R. F. C. Hull, ed. Sir Herbert Read, Michael Fordham, and Gerhard Adler, Bollingen Series XX, vol. 9 (Princeton: Princeton University Press, 1980), p. 130.

26. Ibid., p. 131.

27. Ibid., p. 137.

28. Ibid., p. 131.

29. Ibid., pp. 132–133.

30. Ibid., p. 134.

31. Ibid., p. 121.

Chapter 8

Jung and Reich: The Body as Shadow

Man's body is a problem to him that has not been explained. Not only his body is strange, but also its inner landscape, the memories and dreams. Man's very insides— his self—are foreign to him.

—Ernest Becker, *The Denial of Death*

Strictly speaking, the shadow is the repressed part of the ego and represents what we are unable to acknowledge about ourselves. The body that hides beneath clothes often blatantly expresses what we consciously deny. In the image we present to others, we often do not want to show our anger, our anxiety, our sadness, our constrictedness, our depression, or our need. As early as 1912, Jung wrote: "It must be admitted that the Christian emphasis on spirit inevitably leads to an unbearable depreciation of man's physical side, and thus produces a sort of optimistic caricature of human nature."[1] In 1935, Jung lectured in England about his general theories and, in passing, indicated how the body might stand as the shadow:

We do not like to look at the shadow-side of ourselves; therefore there are many people in our civilized society who have lost their shadow altogether, have lost the third dimension, and with it they have usually lost the body. The body is a most doubtful friend because it produces things we do not like: there are too many things about *the personification of this shadow of the ego.* Sometimes it forms the skeleton in the cupboard, and everybody naturally wants to get rid of such a thing.[2]

Indeed, the body *is* the shadow insofar as it contains the tragic history of how the spontaneous surging of life energy is murdered and rejected in a hundred ways until the body becomes a deadened object. The victory of an overrationalized life is promoted at the expense of the more primitive and natural vitality. For those who can read the body, it holds the record of our rejected side, revealing what we dare not speak, expressing our current and past fears. The body as shadow is predominantly the body as "character," the body as bound energy that is unrecognized and untapped, unacknowledged and unavailable.

Although Jung was a vibrant, tall, physical man, he actually said little about the body. When he built his tower in Bollingen, he returned to a more primitive life, pumping his own water from the well and cutting his own wood. His physicality, spontaneity, and charm indicated a certain comfort and at-homeness in his body. A number of his incidental statements show an attitude toward the body that was in harmony with Reich's ideas but more detached, more metaphoric.

Reich, the one who taught us to observe and work with the body, was direct and concrete. He saw the mind and body as "functionally identical."[3] Reich worked with the psyche as a bodily expression and provided a brilliant alternative and antidote to the sophisticated analytic Vienna psychoanalysts, who at least in the early days were unaware of the power of bodily expression in psychoanalysis. Reich's nature was intense, somewhat rigid, without much tolerance for the play of the metaphysical, literary mind. He was a scientist grounded in what he could see, with an impatient predisposition to dismiss everything else as "mystical," a category he quite early adopted for Jung as he entered Freud's circle in the early 1920s. Later, in *Ether, God, and Devil* (1949), Reich wrote:

> Functional identity as a research principle of orgonomic functionalism is nowhere as brilliantly expressed as in the unity of psyche and soma, of emotion and excitation, of sensation and stimulus. This unity or identity as the base principle of life excludes once and for all any transcendentalism, or even autonomy of the emotions.[4]

Jung, on the other hand, was influenced by Kant, whose theory of knowledge kept Jung philosophically directed primarily to a study of the psyche as a scientist, an empiricist, without concluding that he had hold of Reality. "People mostly don't understand my empirical standpoint," he confessed in a letter to Upton Sinclair. "I am dealing with psychic phenomena, and I am not at all concerned with the naive and, as a rule, unanswerable question whether a thing is historically, i.e., concretely, true or not."[5] It is therefore inevitable that his empirical caution conditions his few statements concerning the relation of mind and body. To Henry Murray he wrote: "Body and spirit are to me mere aspects of the reality of the psyche. Psychic experience is the only immediate experience. Body is as metaphysical as spirit."[6] In another letter, nearly twenty years later, he wrote: "I am personally convinced that our mind corresponds with the physiological life of the body, but the way in which it is connected with the body is for obvious reasons unintelligible. To speculate about such unknowable things is mere waste of time."[7] In the essay "On the Nature of the Psyche," Jung wrote:

> Since psyche and matter are contained in one and the same world, and moreover are in continuous contact with one another and ultimately rest on irrepresentable, transcendental factors, it is not only possible but fairly probable, even, that psyche and matter are two different aspects of one and the same thing."[8]

While there are startling and frequent agreements between them, Reich and Jung approached their work in radically different ways. With such unsettling differences in style and disposition before us, the bringing together of these two systems is an unexpected and awesome exercise. Ironically, it takes place through the theoretical mediation of Freud. Reich and Jung neither talked with each other nor wrote or communicated in any way. Only a few random comments indicate that Reich knew of Jung's existence, and his knowledge of Jung appears opinionated and based on superficial assessment. On the other hand, there is no mention of Reich at all in Jung's writings. But both Reich and Jung returned time and again to compare their concepts with the tenets of Freud. In this unexpected way, a cross-relationship can be established between the concepts of Reich and Jung.

In a paper he wrote in 1939, Jung compared the shadow to Freud's concept of the unconscious. "The shadow," he said, "coincides with the 'personal' unconscious (which corresponds to Freud's conception of the unconscious)."[9] In the preface to the third edition of *The Mass Psychology of Fascism*, which he wrote in August 1942, Reich said that his secondary layer corresponds to Freud's unconscious. Reich explained that fascism emerges out of the second layer of biopsychic structure, which represents three layers of character structure (or deposits of social development) that function autonomously. The surface layer of the average man, according to Reich, is "reserved, polite, compassionate, responsible, conscientious." But the surface layer of "social cooperation is not in contact with the deep biologic core of one's selfhood; it is borne by a second, and intermediate character layer, which consists exclusively of cruel, sadistic, lascivious, rapacious, and envious impulses. It represents the Freudian 'unconscious' or 'what is repressed.'"[10]

Since Jung's "shadow" and Reich's "secondary layer" both correspond to Freud's "unconscious," we can acknowledge at least a rough correspondence between them. As reflected in the body, Reich saw the secondary layer as rigid, chronic contractions of muscle and tissue, a defensive armoring against assault from within and without, a way of shutting down so that the energy flow in the afflicted body was severely reduced. Reich worked directly on the armored layer in the body, in that way releasing the repressed material. The body as the shadow refers, then, to the armored aspect of the body.

In Hans Christian Andersen's fairy tale "The Shadow," a shadow manages to detach itself from its owner, a scholar.[11] The scholar gets along tolerably well, developing a new, somewhat more modest shadow. Some years later, he meets his old shadow, who has become wealthy and eminent. About to be married to a princess, the shadow has the audacity to attempt to hire his old master to be *his* shadow. The scholar attempts to expose his shadow, but the clever shadow has him imprisoned, convincing its betrothed that its shadow has gone mad, and so it is able to remove the man that endangers its love. The fairy tale tells us how the dark and discarded aspects of the ego can coalesce in a forceful unforeseen way and materialize so powerfully as to dominate and reverse the master-servant relationship, a story that demonstrates what Reich would have considered the development of the armored character.

In the strictest sense, then, the body as the shadow represents the body as armored, expressive of what is repressed by the ego. We might also guess that Jung's concept of the persona corresponds to Reich's first layer. "On the surface layer of his personality," wrote Reich (to quote the passage again), "the average man is reserved, polite, compassionate, responsible, conscientious."[12] "The persona," wrote Jung, "is a complicated system of relations between the individual consciousness and society, fittingly enough a kind of mask, designed on the one hand to make a definite impression upon others, and, on the other, to conceal the true nature of the individual."[13] Although Jung's "persona" functions in a more complex way than Reich's "first layer," there is a reasonable correspondence between the two systems. Jung saw the persona as part of a balance between the conscious and unconscious, a sequence of compensations. The more a man plays the strongman for the world, the more inwardly he is compensated by feminine weakness. The less aware he is of the feminine within him, the more likely a man is to project a primitive anima figure on the world, or to be subject to fits, moods, paranoias, hysterias. Reich tended to dismiss the surface layer as inconsequential, whereas Jung attended to the vital interaction between our mask and our inner life.

For Reich, the way to reach the core layer of man was to challenge the secondary shadow layer. The resistance for Reich became a kind of flag, marking the area of armoring, marking the way into the core of man. "In this core, under favorable social conditions, man is an essentially honest, industrious, cooperative, loving, and, if motivated, rationally hating animal."[14]

The equivalence between Jung's shadow concept and Reich's secondary layer is a rough but hardly exact fit. Jung saw the shadow as a part of the core of life within the nature of the God image in the human psyche. The dark side offers us a powerful entrance into the denied life of man. Mephistopheles is able to give Faust back his youth, reestablish his connection to nature, and awaken his heart. Mephistopheles has an ironic charm, a perceptive integrity. Not only a beloved enemy to Faust, he emerges as the double, as the immortal self. For Jung, the value of Hermes

(Mercury), sometimes perceived as a devil figure, is his capacity to pass through the boundaries dividing light and darkness. But for Reich, evil is a chronic mechanism that denies energetic life and is a hindrance to the spontaneous, biologic core of man. The devil never reaches the core level but is the personification of the restricted secondary layer.

After years of work, Reich came to share Freud's therapeutic despair. He had tried to dissolve armor on a mass scale through education and individually in therapy. His three-layer model does not acknowledge a value in the secondary layer, which appears virtually impossible to dissolve completely. These days, it is generally acknowledged among practitioners that everyone needs some armor as protection. Therapy seeks not only to dissolve armor but to introduce flexibility and conscious choice to what had been a rigid, unconscious, defense structure.

While the biological concept of armor has an appropriate specificity in its application to the energetic work with the body, the shadow as the functional equivalent on the psychic level enjoys a range of meaning appropriate to its psychological function. The shadow contains power that has been disowned. The shadow is not to be totally dissolved, nor can it be successfully disowned. The shadow must be related to and integrated even as we acknowledge that some deep core of shadow will never be tamed. The shadow and the double contain not only the dross of our conscious life but our primitive, undifferentiated life force, a promise of the future, whose presence enhances our awareness and strengthens us through the tension of opposites.

Notes

1. C. G. Jung, *Symbols of Transformation: An Analysis of the Prelude to a Case of Schizophrenia*, 2nd ed., trans. R. F. C. Hull, Bollingen Series XX, vol. 5 (Princeton: Princeton University Press, 1956), p. 71.

2. C. G. Jung, *Analytical Psychology: Its Theory and Practice* (New York: Vintage, 1968), p. 23 (italics added).

3. Wilhelm Reich, *The Function of the Orgasm*, trans. Theodore P. Wolfe (New York: Meridian, 1970), p. 241.

4. Wilhelm Reich, *Ether, God, and Devil*, trans. Mary Boyd Higgins and Therese Pol (New York: Farrar, Straus & Giroux, 1973), p. 91.

5. C. G. Jung, "Letter to Upton Sinclair, November 24, 1952," in *C. G. Jung Letters*, trans. R. F. C. Hull, ed. Gerhard Adler and Aniela Jaffé, Bollingen Series XCV, vol. 2 (Princeton: Princeton University Press, 1973), p. 97.

6. C. G. Jung, "Letter to Henry Murray, September 10, 1935," in *C. G. Jung Letters*, vol. 1, p. 200.

7. C. G. Jung, "Letter to D. Cappon, March 15, 1954," in *C. G. Jung Letters*, vol. 2, p. 160.

8. C. G. Jung, *The Structure and Dynamics of the Psyche*, 2nd ed., trans. R. F. C. Hull, Bollingen Series XX, vol. 8 (Princeton: Princeton University Press, 1969), p. 215.

9. C. G. Jung, *The Archetypes and the Collective Unconscious*, trans. R. F. C. Hull, ed. Sir Herbert Read, Michael Fordham, and Gerhard Adler, Bollingen Series XX, vol. 9 (Princeton: Princeton University Press, 1980), p. 284.

10. Wilhelm Reich, *The Mass Psychology of Fascism*, trans. Vincent R. Carfagno (New York: Farrar, Straus & Giroux, 1970), p. xi.

11. Hans Christian Andersen, "The Shadow," in *Hans Christian Andersen: Eighty Fairytales* (New York: Pantheon Press, 1982), p. 193. Also see Otto Rank, *The Double: A Psychoanalytic Study*, trans. and ed. Harry Tucker, Jr. (New York: Meridian, 1971), pp. 10–11.

12. Reich, *Mass Psychology of Fascism*, p. xi.

13. C. G. Jung, *Two Essays on Analytical Psychology*, 2nd ed., trans. R. F. C. Hull, Bollingen Series XX, vol. 7 (Princeton: Princeton University Press, 1972), p. 192.

14. Reich, *Mass Psychology of Fascism*, p. xi.

Chapter 9

The Core,
the Collective
Unconscious,
and Beyond

I seem to have been only like a boy playing on the seashore,
and diverting myself in now and then finding a smoother
pebble or a prettier shell than ordinary, while the great
ocean of truth lay all undiscovered around me.

—Isaac Newton

In a fascinating interview in October 1952, Reich
acknowledged that he agreed with Jung's concept of the collective
unconscious, a concept at which he had also arrived. He said,
however, that he had arrived at his awareness scientifically,
whereas Jung's was mystically conceived:

Jung meant something very important. You know what he
meant? He really meant the energy in the universe, a universal
libido. Freud said it was not scientific. You couldn't measure it on a
Geiger counter as I can. Furthermore, it was mystically conceived.
So Freud was correct in rejecting it. . . .
Oh, yes, now I remember where Jung came into debates. I
tended, then, toward a unification of the instinct theory. That

means that all the many instincts we have—oral, anal, and so on— would have some common root, whereas, in Freud, they stand out as single pillars. I was already on the way to that unification of the partial instincts in a common biological principle. But I had to guard against Jung because he had mystified the whole thing.[1]

Such agreement came only in Reich's later years, after the discovery of orgone energy, when his awareness of the concept had matured and deepened. Certainly, before the discovery of orgone in 1940, Jung's libido concept had for Reich no validity whatsoever. In 1936, on the occasion of Freud's eightieth birthday, Reich wrote disparagingly of Jung's concept: "With Jung, the libido became a meaningless, mystical all-soul concept, the best possible soil for the later Gleichschaltung ['equalizing'] in the Third Reich."[2]

On June 20, 1942, Reich wrote to his old boss and colleague at the Vienna clinic, Dr. Hitschmann, that the libido is orgone energy: "You happen to be one of the very few psychoanalysts who do not recoil from the fact that the libido discovered by our teacher Freud is now both tangible and measurable as biologically efficacious orgone energy. It never fails to amaze me how little the true scientific principle of emotional energy has been grasped and applied."[3] Reich had apparently generalized the libido to encompass the energy of the universe.

The discovery of orgone energy was the major turning point in Reich's life. The man before publication of his orgonomic discoveries, while controversial, was also a counterculture hero, a brilliant, respected teacher, the developer of character analysis and vegetotherapy, the author of *The Mass Psychology of Fascism*, atheistic, and severely anticlerical. He was extroverted, political, arrogant in battle, and living as if unburdened by consequences, while inwardly driven, haunted by critics and by his own inner purposes. For a few years in Sweden, he enjoyed a protection afforded by devoted students. But gradually he moved further away from people toward a life of scientific research. In America he became more guarded, introverted, explosive, wounded—no longer "Willy" but "Reich." Later, in the 1940s, he complained to his friend A. S. Neill, the founder of Summerhill, about having to do therapy, since he preferred to work full-time in the laboratory. The movement into a deeper scientific study was perhaps part of a natural shift in the second half of life and preceded the vicious attacks in the Swedish press concerning his work with sexuality and the origins of life.

Orgone energy was the vehicle by which Reich was able to enter into the grander metaphors regarding humankind. It provided him with a "scientific" justification to finally deal with concepts such as God and the Devil, to feel what the great poets felt, to experience the impact of man swept up in a vast and overreaching nature, to feel at last what the myths had talked about, to experience what the mystics experienced without being one of them. He could even finally understand in some way that Jung's collective unconscious corresponded to his own vast orgone ocean.

For Reich the scientist, so seriously attentive to physical phenomena, the intuitive process of going out of focus to sense and feel what lay beneath or around the immediate grasp of physical phenomena made no sense at all. Such a process was "mystical" rather than scientific, and Reich had no particular vocabulary to include or even identify such an approach to consider it as an alternative. He was brilliant but also awesomely literal, humorless, and concrete. Yet, having entered into the second half of life, he appears to have been drawn toward what was probably his fourth function, the intuitive, the opposite of his sensate focus. So committed to the scientific way, to extroverted, sensate focus, Reich found a way as a scientist to explore the introverted intuitive within himself without knowing it.

In the late 1930s, as he studied movement under the microscope, Reich raised the magnification far beyond the standard optic limit, forcing the image out of focus so that he could watch instead the movement of life. The move out of focus to see was a powerful move into the intuitive, from observer to visionary. Anyone who has used a microscope knows that seeing is an art even in the most rigorous scientific circles, but seeing became for Reich his most critical faculty. He became a seer, a man of visions, who quite often saw what many of his students could not, and his seeing later extended to extremes that others saw as paranoid ideation. Through it all, Reich was able to maintain that he was functioning in a fully scientific manner.

Dr. Reich the seer, the man who stared into the sky for hours and saw orgone energy swirling in identifiable forms, has been judged generally not as a scientist but as a lunatic. Rumors that he was psychotic had pursued him since his break with Freud. The conveniently romantic formula in the culture of old Vienna was that whoever left Freud was cursed in one way or another; Jung was labeled with "mystic," and Reich with "psychotic."

In 1927, Reich went through an emotional breakdown that marked a revolution in his thinking. Like Jung's breakdown, it followed a split with Freud. In the early months of 1927, Reich's conflict with Freud became severe. Reich attributed the break with Freud to character assassination by his analytic enemies, most notably Dr. Paul Federn, and to his own developing political fervor, which Freud did not share. Ilse Ollendorff Reich, his third wife, in her remarkable, dispassionate biography, agrees with Annie Reich, his first wife, who was of the opinion that the most significant factor in the conflict was Freud's refusal to see Reich in therapy: "Freud had become, as I see it in simple terms, a father substitute for Reich. The rejection, as Reich felt it, was intolerable. Reich reacted to this rejection with deep depression."[4]

At about this time, Reich developed tuberculosis, the disease that had killed his father and brother, necessitating his retreat to Davos, Switzerland, for a few months of treatment in a sanitarium. Reich himself describes this period of transition in the most dramatic terms.[5] It dawned upon him that his benign trust in society was ill-placed, that society and human institutions were pathological in their present functioning, a truth that others came to see, he said, in the 1940s. His foundation of trust had suddenly washed away, and he was overwhelmed by the immensity of human illness and treachery. The loss of Freud's support—and the emotional protection that it had afforded—was crushing. Traditional psychoanalysis no longer seemed applicable to a desperate society in turmoil. Reich's Viennese colleagues who disliked him were naively divorced from the politics of the time, hoping to remain unscathed by Nazism by "keeping a low profile."

> The first encounter with human irrationality was an immense shock. I can't imagine how I bore it without going mad. Consider that when I underwent this experience I was comfortably adjusted to conventional modes of thinking. Unaware of what I was dealing with, I landed in the "meat grinder". . . . As if struck by a blow, one suddenly recognizes the scientific futility, the biological senseless-

ness, and the social noxiousness of views and institutions which until that moment had seemed altogether natural and self-evident. It is a kind of eschatological experience so frequently encountered in a pathological form in schizophrenics. I might even voice the belief that the schizophrenic form of psychic illness is regularly accompanied by illuminating insight into the irrationality of social and political mores, primarily in regard to the rearing of small children. . . . The difference between the experience of a schizophrenic and the insight of a strong creative mind lies in the fact that revolutionary insight develops in practice, over long periods of time, often over centuries.[6]

Reich's eschatological experience, his political and personal revolution of thought, was neither understood nor shared by his first wife, Annie, who remained steadfastly loyal to Freud in all matters. In Berlin, where the more politically minded psychoanalysts had been discussing Marxism and psychoanalysis for years under the leadership of Reich's friend Otto Fenichel, Reich settled for a brief time to be in therapy with Sandor Rado. In a grossly unprofessional action, Rado secretly warned Annie Reich that she should leave her husband, whom he considered to be "suffering from an 'insidious psychotic process.'"[7]

In 1933, Otto Fenichel and Edith Gyömröi visited with Reich in Copenhagen, where he lived in exile after Hitler's rise to power. Edith Gyömröi writes:

We met Reich and went to the beach, talking endlessly as we walked. Reich, who meant very much to us at the time, told us about the outline of the book he was then working on. It was the beginning of his Orgone theory. Fenichel and I did not dare to look at each other, and had cold shivers. Then Reich suddenly stopped, and said: "Kinder, wenn ich meiner Sache nicht so sicher ware, wurde es mich anmaten wie eine Skizophrene Fantasie" [Children, if I were not so certain of what I am working on, it would appear to me as a schizophrenic fantasy]. We didn't say anything. Not even on our journey back. It was for us both a great loss and a great sorrow.[8]

Reich's breakthrough in thought in the early 1930s was both radical and unnerving. His direct, radical intervention to release energy in the body, an energy he could measure electrically, made no sense to Fenichel and may have appeared as evidence of mental instability. (Reference to orgone in Gyömröi's account must refer to these early experiments with energy, since there is no other reference to the term "orgone" at so early a date.) Later, when this measurable energy was generalized into orgone energy, others found it easy to dismiss Reich as mad. But his students and collaborators and his last two wives, Elsa Lindenberg and Ilse Ollendorff, did not consider Reich crazy. They found him difficult at times but not psychotic. Nevertheless, we can accept Reich's word that he underwent a profound, dramatic shift in consciousness in 1927, which, as with Jung, determined the course of his thought in the years that followed.

Reich has never been respected as an intuitive, a seer, one who sees past the physical phenomena. For the most part, the Reich who finally had the metaphors to connect to the vast erudition of the human race was an embarrassment to his friends and was viewed as a tragic, broken man who repudiated in his last days the very tenets he had established so vigorously against the pressures of the mass man. In particular, the writings of his last ten years are replete not only with new terminologies, grandiosities, and self-congratulation, but also with the most powerful and moving inner experiences of his relation to life and to nature.

Reich was a true devotee of nature, a Darwinian enthusiast for the future, with an overriding optimism for the power of nature to cleanse itself and move to a better balance with each generation. Unlike an eighteenth-century concept of nature, a mere reflection of God the watchmaker, Darwinian nature, through survival of the fittest, was able to discard the tired, nonfunctional, and inauthentic to produce a healthier, more robust future. Nature's processes are inherently right and the appropriate subject of committed study. The scientist, as devotee and true priest, is filled with a sense of meaning and optimism because nature is boundless, abundant, inexpressible, and a refuge of beauty and wonder. Reich used the word *enigma* in regard to nature, rather than *mystery*, because nature can be known through reason, through science. In Darwinian nature, the future is also a refuge. Alfred Kinsey, another literal-minded, concrete scientist, had something of the same optimism and belief in the underlying goodness of nature. Since we have seen our planet from space, the optimism that nature is limitless in its power to cleanse has come to a sadder but wiser end. Nature evoked in Reich a certain innocent purity that broke through the terrible and bitter disillusionments he felt, a fitting counterbalance to the emotional plague he experienced in society.

In the last ten years of his life, Reich appears to have stepped away from the world, away from the stage of life and into the meadow. His permanent move to Rangely, Maine, in the summer of 1946, supported a deeper connection with nature. His perspective from the meadow is not unlike some of the utterances of Jung. In *Cosmic Superimposition*, Reich wrote:

> Very little of the actual drama of present-day social struggles will appear in these pages. . . . Observed from these meadows, under glittering stars in endless heavens, the show on the stage appears strange. Somehow, the endless heavens on silent nights do not seem in any sort of accord with the show inside the theater or with the subject of the performance. All that belongs to the show seems far off, unreal, and very much out of place if seen from outside the theater building.[9]

Reich's perceptiveness and range of awareness have not been noted by friends or critics. The passage above provides an interesting parallel to one of the poems of Walt Whitman, who also has been accused of grandiosity by those unsympathetic to his expansive merging sense of identity:

> When I heard the learn'd astronomer,
> When the proofs, the figures, were ranged in columns
>   before me,
> When I was shown the charts and diagrams, to add,
>   divide, and measure them,
> When I sitting heard the astronomer where he lectured
>   with much applause in the lecture-room,
> How soon unaccountable I became tired and sick,
> Till rising and gliding out I wander'd off by myself,
> In the mystical moist night-air, and from time to time,
> Look'd up in perfect silence at the stars.[10]

When Reich published *Cosmic Superimposition* in 1951, he had been studying the life of Christ, increasingly identifying with the life and martyrdom. The images lifted him beyond the confines of biology and physics. Indirectly, he described to us, in the following passage, the isolation he felt:

> It does not matter here whether or not human meditation has ever succeeded in lifting the veil. It has at least tried to do so and always outside the realm of human stage performances, be it a theater, a political gathering, or a religious ceremony. When Christ found himself in trouble, he went to meditate completely alone on a meadow or a hill, in silent spaces. And again, something important, though inscrutable, was brought back from the meadow or the mountain onto the human stage.
>
> Every single religious movement in the history of man has tried to bring the message of the emotional depth from the meadow onto the stage inside, in vain.[11]

Like Jung, Reich perceived a functional order relating nature and man, a perception of considerable importance to a scientist. He was finally struck by the "objective functional logic in the natural functions beyond [one's] personal being."[12] Reich continued:

> In the midst of [my] emotional upheaval, [I] began to understand the absolute necessity of the idea of "God" among all peoples, whatever their race or whatever their kind of primitive awareness of this logic in nature may have been. . . . "God," at this point, appeared to be the perfectly logical result of man's awareness of the existence of an objective functional logic in the universe.[13]

Reich found solace in his larger identification with the cosmic orgone ocean; he felt a part of nature, which has its own laws beyond the whims of ego. The movement from stage to meadow is, in fact, a move away from the dominance of the ego to the acceptance of a larger context of the self; it is acceptance of one's place in the larger context of the collective world of nature.

Reich felt that the orgone energy in humanity seeks to become conscious of itself, that there is a hunger in man to become conscious of and know that he is a part of nature, and that there is a relationship as well of microcosm (man) to macrocosm (nature):

> In this light, and only in this, striving for perfecting knowledge has *cosmic* meaning. In penetrating to the greatest depth and the fullest

extent of emotional integration of the self, we not only experience and feel, we also learn to understand, if only dimly, the meaning and functioning of the cosmic orgone ocean, of which we are a tiny part.[14]

That movement from ego to the larger self was described by Jung as a move from the valley to the mountain:

> What, on a lower level, had led to the wildest conflicts and to panicky outbursts of emotion, from the higher level of personality now looked like a storm in the valley seen from the mountaintop. This does not mean that the storm is robbed of its reality, but instead of being in it one is above it. But since, in a psychic sense, we are both valley and mountain, it might seem a vain illusion to deem ourself beyond what is human.[15]

Even in 1912, as a relatively young man, Jung had a profound sense of how nature needs man to be consciously aware of itself. "The world," he wrote, "comes into being when man discovers it, but he only discovers it when he sacrifices his containment in the primal mother, the original state of unconsciousness."[16] Later, in his travels in Africa, Jung had a powerful experience that confirmed in him the sense of man's function in nature, which is to be consciously aware. This is, he thought, an awakening consciousness from the "all-encompassing world-soul Purusha" that represents "the original 'dawn state' of the psyche."[17]

> I can only make a confession of faith: I believe that, after thousands and millions of years, someone had to realize that this wonderful world of mountains and oceans, suns and moons, galaxies and nebulae, plants and animals, *exists*. From a low hill in the Athi plains of East Africa, I once watched the vast herds of wild animals grazing in soundless stillness, as they had done from time immemorial, touched only by the breath of a primeval world. I felt then as if I were the first man, the first creature, to know that all this *is*. The entire world round me was still in its primeval state; it did not know that it *was*. And then, in that one moment in which I came to know, the world sprang into being; without that moment it would never have been. All Nature seeks this goal and finds it fulfilled in man, but only in the most highly developed and most fully conscious man. Every advance, even the smallest, along this path of conscious realization adds that much to the world.[18]

Jung knew that the illness of modern Western culture grew from man's divorce from the world of the archetypes and his rootedness in nature:

> Whether he understands them or not, man must remain conscious of the world of the archetypes, because in it he is still a part of Nature and is connected with his own roots. A view of the world or a social order that cuts him off from the primordial images of life not only is no culture at all but, in increasing degree, is a prison or a stable. If the primordial images remain conscious in some form or other, the energy that belongs to them can flow freely into man.[19]

Reich said in a parallel passage:

> No great poet or writer, no great thinker or artist has ever escaped from this deep and ultimate awareness of being somehow and somewhere rooted in nature at large.[20]

In moving into the impersonal collective world, both Reich and Jung left Freud far behind, caught still upon the stage. Jung wrote of Freud's dilemma:

> It looks as if Freud had got stuck in his own pessimism, cling as he does to his thoroughly negative and personal conception of the unconscious. . . . But pierce the veil of that sickly illusion, and you step out of your narrow, stuffy personal corner into the wide realm of the collective psyche, into the healthy and natural matrix of the human mind, into the very soul of humanity.[21]

Reich had found his way out of the trap that still held Freud. He had broken through the shadow, the personal unconscious, the character structure, the trap in man's emotional structure. He had stepped from the stage to the meadow, and in so doing had suffered losses that alchemists and other adepts had suffered throughout the ages. Reich wrote powerfully about it in *The Murder of Christ*:

> Wherever we turn we find man running around in circles as if trapped and searching the exit in vain and in desperation.
> *It IS possible to get out of a trap.* However, in order to break out of a prison, one first must confess to *being in a prison.* The trap is *man's emotional structure, his character structure. . . . The first thing*

to do is to find the exit out of the trap. . . .
    Where is the exit into the endless open space?
    . . . The keys to the exit are cemented into your own character
armor and into the mechanical rigidity of your body and soul.
    This is the great tragedy. And Christ happened to know it.[22]

Jung said that "in the realm of consciousness we are our own
masters; we seem to be the 'factors' themselves. But if we step
through the door of the shadow, we discover with terror that we
are the objects of unseen factors."[23] Jung also described a path
through the trap into open space:

> The meeting with oneself is, at first, the meeting with one's own
> shadow. The shadow is a tight passage, a narrow door, whose
> painful construction no one is spared who goes down to the deep
> well. But one must learn to know oneself in order to know who one
> is. For what comes after the door is, surprisingly enough, a bound-
> less expanse full of unprecedented uncertainty, with apparently no
> inside and no outside, no above and no below, no here and no
> there, no mine and no thine, no good and no bad. It is the world of
> water, where all life floats in suspension; where the realm of the
> sympathetic system, the soul of everything living, begins; where I
> am indivisibly this and that; where I experience the other in myself
> and the other-than-myself experiences me.[24]

Jung related this collective unconscious world to the body, in
particular to the sympathetic system, which Reich had worked
with and studied extensively:

> The unconscious is the psyche that reaches down from the daylight
> of mentally and morally lucid consciousness into the nervous sys-
> tem that for ages has been known as the "sympathetic." This does
> not govern perception and muscular activity like the cerebrospinal
> system, and thus control the environment; but, though functioning
> without sense-organs, it maintains the balance of life and, through
> the mysterious paths of sympathetic excitation, not only gives us
> knowledge of the innermost life of other beings but also has an
> inner effect upon them.[25]

Although Jung and Reich saw the world in uniquely different
ways, we can acknowledge a rough correspondence between Reich's

"primary layer" and Jung's "persona," Reich's "armor" and Jung's "shadow," and Reich's experience of "orgone" in the core and in nature and Jung's "collective unconscious." Both Reich and Jung felt strongly that nature sought to know itself through the consciousness of man. They experienced the movement from a mundane ego consciousness to a larger self-awareness, a movement from the stage to the meadow, the valley to the mountain. They both felt the need for man to be rooted in the archetypes, in nature. They both could acknowledge the world as presenting a trap to man from which, through special knowledge, he could at some risk escape. And Jung could acknowledge a biological, material base for the collective unconscious, a materiality to symbols.

Notes

1. Wilhelm Reich, *Reich Speaks of Freud* (New York: Farrar, Straus & Giroux, 1967), p. 88, note.

2. Ibid., p. 263.

3. Ibid., p. 227.

4. Ilse Ollendorff Reich, *Wilhelm Reich: A Personal Biography* (New York: St. Martin's Press, 1969), p. 14.

5. Wilhelm Reich, *People in Trouble* (vol. 2 of *The Emotional Plague of Mankind*), trans. Philip Schmitz (New York: Farrar, Straus & Giroux, 1976), p. 7.

6. Ibid.

7. Myron Sharaf, *Fury on Earth: A Biography of Wilhelm Reich* (New York: St. Martin's Press, 1983), p. 193. The allegation about Rado comes from Edith Jacobson, a psychoanalyst.

8. Russell Jacoby, *The Repression of Psychoanalysis: Otto Fenichel and the Political Freudians* (New York: Basic Books, 1983), p. 82, quoting from the manuscript of Edith Rudowyk Gyömröi, "Recollections of Otto Fenichel."

9. Wilhelm Reich, *Cosmic Superimposition*, trans. Mary Boyd Higgins and Therese Pol (New York: Farrar, Straus & Giroux, 1973), pp. 165–166.

10. Walt Whitman, "When I Heard the Learn'd Astronomer," in *Leaves of Grass* (New York: New American Library, 1958), p. 226. For an unsympathetic view of Whitman's "grandiosity," see D. H. Lawrence, *Selected Literary Criticism*, ed. Anthony Beal (New York: Viking Press, 1956), p. 392.

11. Reich, *Cosmic Superimposition*, p. 168.

12. Ibid., p. 283.

13. Ibid. (In this and the preceding passage, Reich refers to himself in the third person.)

14. Ibid., p. 281.

15. C. G. Jung, *Alchemical Studies*, trans. R. F. C. Hull, Bollingen Series XX, vol. 13 (Princeton: Princeton University Press, 1967), p. 15.

16. C. G. Jung, *Symbols of Transformation: An Analysis of the Prelude to a Case of Schizophrenia*, 2nd ed., trans. R. F. C. Hull, Bollingen Series XX, vol. 5 (Princeton: Princeton University Press, 1956), p. 417.

17. Ibid.

18. C. G. Jung, *The Archetypes and the Collective Unconscious*, trans. R. F. C. Hull, ed. Sir Herbert Read, Michael Fordham, and Gerhard Adler, Bollingen Series XX, vol. 9 (Princeton: Princeton University Press, 1980), pp. 95–96.

19. Ibid., p. 93.

20. Reich, *Cosmic Superimposition*, p. 280.

21. C. G. Jung, *The Practice of Psychotherapy: Essays on the Psychology of the Transference and Other Subjects*, 2nd ed., trans. R. F. C. Hull, Bollingen Series XX, vol. 16 (Princeton: Princeton University Press, 1966), p. 35.

22. Wilhelm Reich, *The Murder of Christ* [vol. 1 of *The Emotional Plague of Mankind*] (New York: Simon & Schuster, 1953), pp. 3–5 (italics added).

23. Jung, *Archetypes*, p. 23.

24. Ibid., pp. 21–22.

25. Ibid., pp. 19–20.

Chapter 10

Science and Mysticism

To prayer I think I go
I go to prayer—
Along a darkened corridor of woe
And down a stair
In every step of which I am abased.
I wear a halter-rope about the waist.
I bear a candle end put out with haste.
For such as I there is reserved a crypt
That from its stony arches having dripped
Has stony pavement in a slime of mould.
There I will throw me down an unconsoled
And utter loss,
And spread out in the figure of a cross.—
Oh, if religion's not to be my fate
I must be spoken to and told
Before too late!

—Robert Frost

In the seventeenth century, Protestants and Catholics, when they were not persecuting Jews, killed each other, thinking they had hold of an absolute truth, a revelation that set them apart and justified atrocity against other people. By the eighteenth century, some men passionately espoused reason, which provided a vantage point from which to evaluate the righteous absolute proclamations of opposing forces. The appeal to reason and common sense, the judgment of educated men, allowed a humanistic platform to evolve that became the inspired vision of a developing science. To some degree, science was coupled with a consideration for the equality of all men, a modest acknowledgment that one did not possess an absolute truth but was profoundly limited by only relative and partial awareness, and that that awareness needed to be validated by the impartial questioning of others. This enlightened principle unseated the religious absolutism of the past, which too often served selfish, powerful men, and threw any private revelations into question.

Reasonable men devised a reasonable god, just as bloodthirsty men obediently followed a vengeful god. Some kind of traditional god died in the nineteenth century, and an evolutionary man was born. People believed in the charismatic force of reason. Thus, the twentieth century was not prepared for the unleashing of a violent irrationality, dark currents of the unconscious that swallowed the small island of culture in a single gulp of war.

By the twentieth century, the marriage of Church and State had sufficiently broken down in Western culture so that the religious experience, the private revelation, was not always packaged with political or personal gain. Instead of the Church carrying the sword, science became the new murderer. Against this background, arguments concerning science and mysticism fell into renewed confusion.

What relationship was one to form between the reasonable and the irrational in one's nature? Was the unconscious a swamp that should be drained and turned to some use, or was it to be preserved as a wildlife sanctuary? What was a scientific or a mystical attitude? Which was the killer and which the savior? Was one's relation to nature scientific or mystical?

Freud, Jung, and Reich were each determined to resolve for themselves the seeming polarity of science and mysticism. More specifically, there was confusion concerning the appropriate balance between a biological framework and a philosophically based psychology. Freud, trained as a research scientist and influenced by nineteenth-century materialism, rejected mystical experience, which he explained with psychological hypotheses. For him, a more serious issue was to establish psychoanalysis as a credible science with rules and concepts of its own, not merely borrowed from biology. This transformation of psychology as a science was catalyzed for Freud by his profound relationship with Wilhelm Fliess. The ideas of Freud, Fliess, and the sexologists were all part of a major conceptual offshoot of the Darwinian revolution.

Frank Sulloway, in *Freud: Biologist of the Mind*, suggests that Freud's withdrawal from a biological framework had complex roots. Sulloway uncovers the pervasive influence of Fliess on the work of psychoanalysis, resulting in Fliess's painful break with Freud. Their friendship in the 1890s provided them with a free and open sharing of scientific ideas, and it was Fliess who first convinced Freud of the bisexuality of man.[1]

So long as Freud held to the seduction theory as the traumatic cause for neurotic illness, he was unthreatened by the powerful influence of Fliess and his sexual biology. "We share like the two beggars," Freud said, "one of whom allotted himself the province of Posen: you take the biological, I the psychological."[2] Once he had abandoned his seduction theory, however, Freud's scientific relationship with Fliess became uncomfortably competitive. He wanted to use Fliess's ideas in his own way. "At the heart of the altered relationship between the two scientists," says Sulloway, "was the issue of how much biological reductionism was necessary and appropriate in Freud's increasingly genetic conception of human thought and behavior."[3] While the biological relationship to the psyche was established in Fliess's mind, Freud had remained tentative. To Fliess's questioning, he responded on September 22, 1898:

> I am not in the least in disagreement with you, and have no desire at all to leave the psychology hanging in the air with no organic basis. But, beyond a feeling of conviction [that there must be such a basis], I have nothing, either theoretical or therapeutic, to work on, and so I must behave as if I were confronted by psychological factors only. I have no idea yet why I cannot yet fit [the psychological and the organic] together.[4]

Freud saw himself in "his growing psychological self-image" as "pitted against the established medical theories," which were somatic and physiological; "and in contrast, . . . Freud erected a sophisticated psychobiology of mind, which seemed to him like a pure psychology that had finally revealed the misguided fallacies of the organicist paradigm of mind."[5]

As his psychology developed, it became necessary for Freud to separate it from the parent discipline in order to develop its own unique structures, lest it remain forever a mere child restricted to the approval and intellectual limitations of the parent.[6]

Although Freud relinquished any attempt to base psychology in neurophysiology, his theory was "suffused with his evolutionary conception of life. . . . Above all, it was Freud's continued appeal to biological assumptions that justified his personal conviction that he had finally created a universally valid theory of human thought and behavior."[7]

However, at the same time that Freud was separating psychology from the other sciences, he did not want it to become the stepchild of philosophy or religion. He even imagined himself as exempt from a mystical turn of mind. Erich Neumann points out that Freud had a fundamental unconsciousness about his own spiritual heritage as a Jew. In a letter to Karl Abraham, Freud wrote: "We Jews have an easier time, having no mystical element."[8] Somehow, Freud could project the religious attitude onto non-Jews and forget, as Neumann notes, "that the Jews are the religious people par excellence and have, in the kabbala and in Hassidism, produced the most important mystical ideas and movements."[9]

Reich could never understand why Freud was reluctant to embrace his biological solutions to the issue of sexuality, instead preferring to indulge in theoretical speculation, which to Reich seemed untenable in a clinical setting. In the late 1920s, Freud was in fact moving toward a philosophy less dependent on therapeutic cures and more concerned with a way of being in the world—an attitude that was at once resigned, stoic, empathetic, ironic, and detached. Reich was unable to grasp this attitude of Freud as an old man; he was young and believed in science, and Freud stirred him to a sense of valor and honor in a great cause. "One belonged," said Reich, "to an elite of scientific fighters and formed a front against quackery in the therapy of neurosis.[10] The history of science was pure and valid and gave meaning to his life:

> The history of science is a long chain of continuation and elaboration, shaping and reshaping, creation and criticism, renewed shaping and reshaping, and new creation. It is a hard, long road, and we are only at the beginning of this history. Including long empty spaces, it stretches over only about 2,000 years. It always goes ahead, and, fundamentally, never backwards. The pace of life

becomes accelerated, and life becomes more complicated. Honest scientific pioneer work has always been its leader and always will be. Aside from this, everything is hostile to life. This places an obligation upon us.[11]

But as a member of the continuing scientific community, one is granted immortality of sorts. Reich felt that he, in particular, was special to Freud, since the two of them were the only psychoanalysts who had valid scientific training.[12]

Reich felt that Freud had the capacity to think "in a natural, scientific way" rather than just psychologically. But "the psychoanalytic association fell completely short" because no one else was able to think as a scientist until Reich joined the group.[13] However, as a scientist, Freud did not see the need to relate to politics or the social condition, whereas Reich felt an obligation as a scientist to be socially conscious. "'Politically,' he [Freud] always said, 'I'm a scientist, I have nothing to do with politics,' and since politics was hooked up with sociology, I said, 'that's an impossible standpoint.' You can't be apolitical in a situation such as the world was in."[14]

Reich initially considered religion as the great deceiver of men. A major cause of neurosis, he thought, was the sexual suppression promoted by the Church and carried out in families. Childhood taboos and punishments around masturbation, Reich said, were supported by religion, whose "mystical contagion" derived from unrecognized repressed sexual energy. "Mysticism's function is clearly articulated; to divert attention from daily misery, 'to liberate from the world,' the purpose of which is to prevent a revolt against the real causes of one's misery."[15]

In his later scientific work, Reich was under attack by scientists who were mechanistic in their approach, unwilling to explore "life" because it crossed over too many secure barriers of so-called science. Like a hunter after the fox, the hounds yelping hot in pursuit, Reich jumped his neighbors' fences and raced through their scientific gardens with no attention to etiquette or propriety. Cancer research, physics, and astronomy were so many open fields through which to pursue the fox. There was no time to win the proper credentials, to observe the ritualistic obeisances to the scientific landowners.

Reich was at war with scientific territorialism as well as with the inner mechanistic attitude that so tenaciously restricted scientists' methods and fields of observation. Scientific validation in areas where subjective and emotional factors were present and acknowledged represented for Reich a more natural, flexible approach, which he called functionalism. This approach avoided the rigidities of mechanism and the flights of fancy of ungrounded disembodied mysticism. Functionalism did not presume an objectivity that was not there, nor did it avoid inclusive modes of thought. Like Jung, Reich needed a definition of science that allowed him to follow the fox unhindered. "Nature is imprecise," he argued. "Nature does not operate mechanically but functionally."[16] Functionalism does not overlook emotions. Functionalism is not abstract but "tangible, full, pulsating, and simultaneously demonstrable and measurable."[17] Mechanistic science kills life, stains it, puts it under the microscope, and assumes that what the observer sees is still "life." Functionalism adapts its methods to study the living:

> Research without errors is impossible. All natural research is, and always was, groping, "irregular," unstable, flexible, forever corrective, in flux, uncertain and insecure, and yet in contact with real processes. For these real processes, in spite of all their basic unifying laws, are variable in the highest degree, free in the sense of being irregular, unpredictable, and unrepeatable.[18]

Years later, in the early 1950s, Reich was still using the word *mysticism* to represent a withdrawal or separation, a retreat from one's body, one's true life, and humanity:

> For the mystic, a soul "lives" in the body. There is no connection between body and soul except for the fact that the soul influences the body and vice versa. To the mystic (and to the mechanist, if he is aware of any emotional factors at all), body and soul are rigidly separated through interrelated realities.[19]

A mystic simply experiences body sensations in a distorted way because of armoring. *Mysticism* here means, in the literal sense, a change of sensory impressions and organ sensations into something unreal and beyond this world.[20]

Reich said that primitive man projected his own sensations onto nature, animating them, giving human character to the sun and trees, but that modern man projects perverted, distorted sensations. Reich had worked for a long time with a schizophrenic woman patient whose system of projecting another world eventually came to light, providing an interesting parallel to and explanation of the mystical response. Reich concluded that the mystic, whose psychological structure is close to that of the schizoid character,[21] experiences his organ sensations as if through a distorting mirror:

> In this way a unified ego gradually crystallizes from the chaos of internal and external perceptions; it begins to become aware of the boundary between ego and outer world. If now the child experiences a severe shock in this period of orienting himself, the boundaries remain blurred, vague or uncertain. Stimuli from the outer world may then be perceived as inner experiences, or, conversely, inner perceptions may be experienced as coming from the outer world. . . . The beginning of the loss of reality testing in schizophrenia lies in the patient's misinterpretation of sensations arising from his own body. We are all simply a complicated electric machine which has a structure of its own and is in interaction with the energy of the universe. . . . Today I know that mental patients experience this harmony without any boundary between ego and outer world. And that the Babbits have no idea of this harmony, feeling their beloved egos, sharply circumscribed, to be the center of the universe.[22]

Jung also studied the relation of madness to spiritual vision. While Reich defined mysticism in his own way, making it wrong, he nevertheless moved into experiencing what others might describe as "mystical." But he called his own process functionalism. Reich was having experiences through what he considered science that hitherto had been the province only of the spiritually inclined. In *Ether, God, and Devil*, he went so far as to outline his misconceptions of the past and suggest that since he had been wrong in the past, it was quite possible that he was wrong at present. "I know," he said, "human erring from my own experience. I, too, have joined in the shouting, 'Guilty! Guilty!'"[23]

Reich once blamed religion as solely responsible for human suffering, but he came to see religion as a symptom, not the cause.

As a socialist, he had blamed capitalism for the human condition. As a proponent of Freud, he had once held that the unconscious was evil and responsible for human misery. But, he said, he remained mobile. Now he held "human distress to be the pathology of human structure, which in turn lies in its armoring,"[24] although that also may be merely a mechanism. Reich finally postulated what every good prelate has stated for centuries, but Reich had his own terminology for it: that man's distress may be attributed to his relationship to the "cosmic energy that governs him":

> The answer lies somewhere in that area of our existence which has been so heavily obscured by organized religion and put out of our reach. Hence, it probably lies in the relation of the human being to the cosmic energy that governs him.[25]

Reich somehow thought that all religious experience was simply a desperate crutch, a reaching after a lost experience of life. If the body were released from armoring, life would be immediately present and would be the answer to religious quest and hunger.

Reich came to believe that he had discovered the universal life energy, once thought of as ether, and that he could see it and measure it with a Geiger counter. He took solace in sensing his connection to this vast cosmic orgone ocean. He began to see that his experience paralleled experiences of spiritual people; however, he discounted their methods as "mystical," whereas he had arrived at his experience scientifically, functionally. He talked of this vast orgone ocean in the same way that Eastern mystics have felt the presence of Brahma. Reich felt the mystical longing to be a part of the underlying presence, but of course in his own language:

> Orgastic longing, which plays such an enormous role in animal life, now appears to express this "striving beyond one's own self," this "yearning" to escape from the narrow confines of one's own organism.[26]

Reich went on to express from his own experience what the great mystics experienced, the hungering of "God" to return home to itself, the urge of life to move irresistibly toward self-awareness, the hunger of life to know:

There lives in and strives in us a thirst for knowledge stronger than any philosophical thought, be it life-positive or life-negative. This burning urge to know can be felt like a stretching out of our senses beyond the material framework of our body, enabling us to understand what is rational in the metaphysical view of existence.[27]

What Reich experienced was a direct, intuitive apprehension of God, Life, Nature, Brahma, Cosmic Orgone, or whatever one wants to call it. R. D. Ranade, the author of *Mysticism in India*, has defined mysticism in a somewhat different way than Reich:

Mysticism denotes that attitude of mind which involves a direct, immediate, first-hand intuitive apprehension of God. When mysticism is understood in this sense, there is no reason why it should be taken to signify any occult or mysterious phenomena as is occasionally done.[28]

How, then, are we to distinguish between a valid and an unproductive mysticism? Erich Neumann, a Jungian, in his remarkable essay "Mystical Man," distinguishes between two kinds of mysticism. Uroboros mysticism is a longing for a womb-like return to an illusory paradise, a failure to ground oneself in the world, very much the nihilistic mysticism that Reich deplored. The second kind of mysticism, however, experiences phenomena in such a way that the mystic returns transformed, his consciousness enriched. It is in the nature of the creative man to push past the ego to the borderline of non-ego, to spontaneity, the unknown, the numinous.[29] The act is courageous and life-affirming, very much like Reich's own creative experiences. As a scientist, Reich seems to have been unaware that the physics of relativity and quantum theory postulated a view of man in the universe in harmony with Eastern mysticism; and yet, his concept of functionalism incorporates similar attitudes concerning scientific participation in nature. Fritjof Capra has written:

Modern physics . . . has made a great step toward the world-view of the Eastern mystics in atomic theory. Quantum theory has abolished the notion of fundamentally separated objects, has introduced the concept of the participator to replace that of the observer, and may even find it necessary to include the human consciousness in its description of the world. It has come to see the universe as an interconnected web of physical and mental relations whose parts are defined only through their connections to the whole.[30]

Unlike Reich, Jung was attentive to the implications of modern physics. He co-authored a book with the physicist Wolfgang Pauli.[31] Also, Jung translated the spiritual process into psychological terms and subjected it to the rigors of intellect and ego. His studies ranged over Eastern religions and into the past, into Gnosticism, and finally into alchemy, which for Jung became the bridge that linked the early Gnostics with present-day Western man. Alchemy became a way for Jung to study the interrelationship of psyche and matter. In *Symbols of Transformation*, which was published in 1912 and precipitated his break with Freud, Jung distinguished between two kinds of thinking:

> We have, therefore, two kinds of thinking: direct thinking, and dreaming or fantasy-thinking. The former operates with speech elements for the purpose of communication, and is difficult and exhausting; the latter is effortless, working as it were spontaneously, with the contents ready to hand, and guided by unconscious motives. The one produces innovations and adaptation, copies reality, and tries to act upon it; the other turns away from reality, sets free subjective tendencies, and as regards adaptation, is unproductive.
>
> As I have indicated above, history shows that directed thinking was not always as developed as it is today. The clearest expression of modern directed thinking is science and the techniques fostered by it. Both owe their existence simply and solely to energetic training in directed thinking.[32]

Directed thinking, the unique development of Western culture, is represented by science, and it was this very tool that Jung brought to bear in all the areas of religious life that had previously been the province of mysticism. (Reich's functionalism was a significant parallel to Jung's empiricism.) Jung was unwilling to be restricted by a rigidly biological system or to dismiss vast areas of mankind's learning as unscientific and unworthy of study, nor did he plunge into religious practice and abandon the power of the ego, the presence of the questioning consciousness. In his early days, Reich dismissed Jung for generalizing the concept of libido. Jung, he thought, had generalized the concept to such an extent as to make it completely lose its meaning of *sexual* energy, and ended up with the "collective unconscious."[33] But Jung saw his action in another way. He felt that, for Freud (and this opinion could certainly have applied to Reich as well), sexuality was a *"numinosum,"* with "deeper elements reverberating within him" evident from the emotionality with which he spoke about sexuality. Basically, says Jung, Freud "wanted to teach—or so it seemed to me—that regarded from within, sexuality included spirituality and had an intrinsic meaning. But his concretistic terminology was too narrow to express this idea. He gave me the impression that at bottom he was working against his own goal and against himself."[34]

Jung said that he went on to explore in his work the spiritual aspect of the sexual "and its numinous meaning, and thus to explain what Freud was so fascinated by but was unable to grasp. . . . Sexuality is of the greatest importance as the expression of the chthonic spirit." That spirit is the "other face of God, the dark side of the God-image."[35]

In Jung's early writing, while he was still in agreement with Freud, he related libido to the formation of the God-image in the psyche:

> I am therefore of the opinion that, in general, psychic energy or libido creates the God-image by making use of *archetypal patterns,* and that man in consequence *worships the psychic force active within him as something divine.* We thus arrive at the objectionable conclusion that, from the psychological point of view, the God-image is a real but subjective phenomenon.[36]

Jung described how archetypal psychology had involved him far beyond the parameters of conventional science, but how psychology had no self-consistent mathematics or Archimedean point from which to evaluate itself:

> The problems of analytical psychology, as I have tried to outline them here, led to conclusions that astonished even me. I fancied I was working along the best scientific lines, establishing facts, observing, classifying, describing causal and functional relations, only to discover in the end that I had involved myself in a net of reflections which extend far beyond natural science and ramify into the fields of philosophy, theology, comparative religion, and the humane sciences in general. This transgression, as inevitable

as it was suspect, has caused me no little worry. Quite apart from my personal incompetence in these fields, it seemed to me that my reflections were suspect also in principle, because I am profoundly convinced that the "personal equation" has a telling effect upon the results of psychological observation. The tragic thing is that psychology has no self-consistent mathematics at its disposal, but only a calculus of subjective prejudices.[37]

Jung went on to describe in greater detail the dilemma that psychology faces in regard to itself in a scientific framework. "There is," he said, "no medium for psychology to reflect itself in; it can only portray itself in itself, and describe itself."[38] And so Jung conducted a study of man with no fixed reference points outside the psyche of man:

> The psyche is the world's pivot: not only is it the one great condition for the existence of a world at all, it is also an intervention in the existing natural order, and no one can say with certainty where this intervention will finally end. It is hardly necessary to stress the dignity of the psyche as an object of natural science.[39]

Jung was sufficiently aware of the new physics to relate the phenomenology of the psyche to Eastern philosophy and quantum theory. Man's relation to the phenomenal world had changed radically, and even the physicist was no longer able to stand outside nature and observe it. There was no longer a place in the new space-time world for the scientist to be an objective observer:

> Experience has shown that light and matter both behave like separate particles and also like waves. This paradoxical conclusion obliges us to abandon, on the plane of atomic magnitudes, a causal description of nature in the ordinary space-time system, and in its place to set up invisible fields of probability in multidimensional spaces, which do in fact represent the state of our knowledge at present. Basic to this abstract scheme of explanation is a conception of reality that takes account of the uncontrollable effects the observer has upon the system observed, the result being that reality forfeits something of its objective character and that a subjective element attaches to the physicist's picture of the world.[40]

The subjective and objective approaches were no longer poles apart—the science that Jung practiced was no longer removed from the startling innovation being made in the heart of the scientific world. The inside of man, his psyche, Jung discovered from Phile-mon, had objective contents. A person could step inside an evolu-tionary objective psychic world, or a world of collective contents and representations, and struggle to determine its contents as a participant in the same way as the physicist. There was in Jung's mind a way in which psyche and matter were perhaps different aspects of the same thing. Physics had certainly destroyed the solidity of the physical world.

Jung described himself as an empiricist and a phenomenolo-gist. His empirical approach might have been a clever facade to shield himself from the judgments of others and give himself "scientific" validity, but Jung had a far deeper commitment to the directed thinking of the mind. It provided him with a powerful anchor in the ego from which he could return after extraordinary excursions into Eastern religion, the thinking of the primitive mind, atomic physics, the psychosis of patients, and his own unconscious. He did not understand how the East could give up the ego, and he felt that for the Westerner the loss would be irrepara-ble. In a related experience, during his journey to Africa in 1925, he had a dream suggesting that if he stayed longer he was in danger of being taken over by "the dark continent," "going black," and being swallowed up by his own awakened primitive side. Interest-ingly enough, Jung's reluctance to give up the ego in the Eastern process is shared by physicists who are faced in some way with a similar choice. On this point, Fritjof Capra has commented:

> The mystics are not satisfied with a situation analogous to atomic physics, where the observer and the observed cannot be separated, but can still be distinguished. They go much further, and in deep meditation they arrive at a point where the distinction between observer and observed breaks down completely, where subject and object fuse into a unified undifferentiated whole. Thus the Upanishads say:
>
>> Where there is a duality, as it were, there one sees another; there one smells another; there one tastes another. . . . But where everything has become just one's own self, then whereby and whom would one see? Then whereby and whom would one smell? Then whereby and whom would one taste?

This, then, is the final apprehension of the unity of all things. It is reached—so the mystics tell us—in a state of consciousness where one's individuality dissolves into an undifferentiated oneness, where the world of the senses is transcended and the notion of "things" is left behind.[41]

Over the years, Jung received many letters from clergy. Some were appreciative of his work, while others were disturbed by his failure to proclaim his "faith." He wrote to Pastor Ernst Jahn:

When I speak of God, I always speak as a psychologist, as I have expressly emphasized in many places in my books; for the psychologist the God-image is a psychological fact. He cannot say anything about the metaphysical reality of God because that would far exceed the limits of the theory of knowledge. As an empiricist I know only the images originating in the unconscious which man makes of God, or which, to be more accurate, are made of God in the unconscious; and these images are undoubtedly very relative.[42]

To a Herr Irminger, he wrote:

First of all, I would like to thank you for having taken so much trouble to show me how the Catholic doctrine completes and perfects my psychological writings. You also wonder—rightly, from your point of view—why I don't declare my belief in God and return to the bosom of the Church. . . . My dear Sir! My *pursuit is science*, not apologetics and not philosophy, and I have neither the capacity nor the desire to found a religion. *My interest is scientific, yours evangelical.* . . . As a scientist I have to guard against believing that I am in possession of a final truth.[43]

Reich complained of being called mystical because he explored areas that had been the prerogative of religion. He heatedly defended his right as a scientist to investigate "mysticism" in a functional way. In a parallel manner, Jung experienced vicious attacks and defended himself as an empiricist:

Critics have sometimes accused me outright of "philosophical" or even "theological" tendencies, in the belief that I want to explain everything "philosophically" and that my psychological views are "metaphysical." But I use certain philosophical, religious and historical material for the exclusive purpose of *illustrating* the psychological facts.[44]

The development of a self-consistent psychology at once scientific and unrestricted in exploration has been an elusive goal. But psychology cannot be governed by the rules of other disciplines. It has had to develop its own unique standards of evaluation. And Jung, who embarked so long ago from what looked like the solid shores of a rational scientific world, found that his own journey without known parameters was paralleled by the thinkers of modern physics. Science itself is a "myth" of our time, and into this myth Jung translated the ancient myths:

> Psychology, as one of the many expressions of psychic life, operates
> with ideas which in their turn are derived from archetypal struc-
> tures and thus generate a somewhat more abstract kind of myth.
> Psychology therefore translates the archaic speech of myth into a
> modern mythology—not yet, of course, recognized as such—which
> constitutes one element of the myth "science."[45]

In their struggles to declare a scientific psychology separate from metaphysics, Freud, Reich, and Jung accomplished significant goals. Freud carved out a place for modern psychology separate from biology, philosophy, and religion, which threatened to engulf the new discipline. Reich, through his attention to the body, was able to relate the psyche to the biological experience of man. Reich's functionalism, like Jung's empiricism, gave him a scientific latitude to explore experience that by its very nature dissolved any clear boundaries between the observer and the phenomena observed. Jung, in his search to understand the relationship between psyche and matter, was able to relate psychology to modern physics and to spiritual disciplines. Jung saw that spirituality, like sexuality, rooted in the unconscious, was inseparably the human condition, and that one might experience mystical states without abandoning any key functioning such as critical intelligence. As twentieth-century explorers, all three men were faced with the task of sorting out the rational and irrational and forming a new and consistent attitude toward the violent and benign in the unconscious of twentieth-century man.

Notes

1. Frank J. Sulloway, *Freud: Biologist of the Mind—Beyond the Psychoanalytic Legend* (New York: Basic Books, 1979), p. 183.

2. Quoted in ibid., p. 217.

3. Ibid., p. 217.

4. Sigmund Freud, *Origins of Psychoanalysis: Letters to Wilhelm Fliess, Drafts and Notes, 1887–1902*, ed. Marie Bonaparte, Anna Freud, and Ernst Kris, trans. Eric Mosbacher and James Strachey (New York: Basic Books, 1954), p. 264.

5. Sulloway, *Freud*, p. 422.

6. Ibid., p. 426.

7. Ibid.. p. 419.

8. Erich Neumann, *Creative Man: Five Essays: Kafka/Trakl/Chagall/Freud/Jung*, trans. Eugene Rolfe, Bollingen Series LXI, vol. 2 (Princeton: Princeton University Press, 1982), p. 238.

9. Ibid.

10. Wilhelm Reich, *The Function of the Orgasm*, trans. Theodore P. Wolfe (New York: Meridian, 1970), p. 31.

11. Ibid., p. 18.

12. Wilhelm Reich, *Reich Speaks of Freud* (New York: Farrar, Straus & Giroux, 1967), p. 4.

13. Ibid., p. 121.

14. Ibid., p. 83.

15. Wilhelm Reich, *The Mass Psychology of Fascism*, trans. Vincent R. Carfagno (New York: Farrar, Straus & Giroux, 1970), p. 126.

16. Wilhelm Reich, *Ether, God, and Devil*, trans. Mary Boyd Higgins and Therese Pol (New York: Farrar, Straus & Giroux, 1973), p. 83.

17. Ibid., p. 95.

18. Ibid., p. 84.

19. Ibid., p. 91.

20. Ibid., p. 88.

21. Wilhelm Reich, *Character Analysis*, 3rd ed., trans. Theodore P. Wolfe (New York: Farrar, Straus & Giroux, 1949), p. 401.

22. Reich, *Function of the Orgasm*, pp. 24–25.

23. Reich, *Ether, God, and Devil*, p. 46.

24. Ibid., p. 47.

25. Ibid.

26. Wilhelm Reich, *Cosmic Superimposition*, trans. Mary Boyd Higgins and Therese Pol (New York: Farrar, Straus & Giroux, 1973), p. 222.

27. Ibid., pp. 278–279.

28. R. D. Ranade, *Mysticism in India: The Poet-Saints of Maharashtra* (Albany, N.Y.: State University of New York Press, 1983), p. xiii.

29. Erich Neumann, "Mystical Man," trans. Ralph Manheim, *Spring 1961* (1961): 9–49.

30. Fritjof Capra, *The Tao of Physics* (New York: Bantam, 1976), p. 129.

31. C. G. Jung and W. Pauli, *The Interpretation of Nature and the Psyche* (New York: Pantheon, 1955).

32. C. G. Jung, *Symbols of Transformation: An Analysis of the Prelude to a Case of Schizophrenia*, 2nd ed., trans. R. F. C. Hull, Bollingen Series XX, vol. 5 (Princeton: Princeton University Press, 1956), pp. 18–19.

33. Reich, *Reich Speaks of Freud*, p. 263.

34. C. G. Jung, *Memories, Dreams, Reflections*, rev. ed., trans. Richard and Clara Winston, ed. Aniela Jaffé (New York: Pantheon, 1973), p. 152.

35. Ibid., p. 168.

36. Jung, *Symbols of Transformation*, p. 86.

37. C. G. Jung, *The Structure and Dynamics of the Psyche*, 2nd ed., trans. R. F. C. Hull, Bollingen Series XX, vol. 8 (Princeton: Princeton University Press, 1969), p. 216.

38. Ibid., p. 217.

39. Ibid.

40. Ibid., p. 229.

41. Capra, *Tao of Physics*, p. 128

42. C. G. Jung, "Letter to Pastor Ernst Jahn, September 7, 1935," in *C. G. Jung Letters*, trans. R. F. C. Hull, ed. Gerhard Adler and Aniela Jaffé, Bollingen Series XCV, vol. 1: 1906–1950 (Princeton: Princeton University Press, 1973), p. 195.

43. C. G. Jung, "Letter to Herr Irminger, September 22, 1944," in *C. G. Jung Letters*, vol. 1, p. 346.

44. Jung, *Structure and Dynamics*, p. 278.

45. C. G. Jung, *The Archetypes and the Collective Unconscious*, trans. R. F. C. Hull, ed. Sir Herbert Read, Michael Fordham, and Gerhard Adler, Bollingen Series XX, vol. 9 (Princeton: Princeton University Press, 1980), p. 179.

Chapter 11

Alchemy and Orgone

I placed a jar in Tennessee,
and round it was, upon a hill.
It made the slovenly wilderness
Surround that hill.

The wilderness rose up to it,
and sprawled around, no longer wild.
The jar was round upon the ground
and tall and of a port in air.

It took dominion everywhere
The jar was gray and bare.
It did not give of bird or bush,
like nothing else in Tennessee.

—Wallace Stevens, "Anecdote of the Jar"

According to Marie-Louise von Franz, the psyche/matter issue is not solved. She and Jung felt that probably the unconscious has a material aspect, and that is how the unconscious can know about itself as matter. Alchemy is not merely an archaeological play toy, but deals directly with the relationship of the psyche and matter, as yet an unsolved, engrossing mystery.[1]

Both Jung and Reich were alchemists. Jung once told a story in this connection that was indirectly about himself, but it can also be thought of, with some modifications, as a story about Reich. It is about an old hermit who lives in a cave and is considered by the curious to be a sorcerer. Disciples gather around him hoping to learn his secrets, but the old man, who meditates a great deal, is a seeker himself, searching out what he does not know and grasping for what lies beyond his meditations. As an aid to his search, he takes to drawing diagrams with chalk. After many struggles, he feels some satisfaction one day when he draws a circle and then adds a quadrangle within it. As Jung continues the tale:

> His disciples were curious; but all they could make out was that the old man was up to something, and they would have given anything to know what he was doing. But when they asked him: "What are you doing there?" he made no reply. Then they discovered the diagrams on the wall and said: "That's it!"—and they all imitated the diagrams. But in so doing they turned the whole process upside down, without noticing it: they anticipated the result in the hope of making the process repeat itself that had led to that result. This is how it happened then and how it still happens today.[2]

The queer old man is not outwardly directed at all. He is a teacher only secondarily. His primary concern is to know what it is that he does not know—something that is always present, always happening. He is an old man searching out his connectedness to a universal present. In his lifelong journey he has acquired powers, and then disciples who are focused on his particular powers, something quite separate from and secondary to his inner longing and his lifelong commitment. Rather than seeking to know what they do not know and finding their inner connection to what is always happening now, his disciples are more involved in learning his "sorcery," which is no doubt of great value, but not the same as embarking on their own inner journey. Therefore, the discovery of the mandalas does not come organically for them (as a spontaneous outpouring of the unconscious) so that they feel the truth of true form spontaneously; instead it becomes something they learn but have never been driven to by themselves. They have not paid the full price for inner learning, and so remain unenlightened.

Reich showed us a similar state of being in *Cosmic Superimposition*. He drew out the images he observed in nature and in the sky, illustrating the cosmic superimposition of one form upon another. He had studied the forms of nature for years, and he drew diagrams, but others were not able to follow him. He was in his own world; he saw what others did not see, and they did not know how to follow him there. Thus, he wrote:

The cosmic orgone ocean, which has been surveyed in some detail in this book, pursues its eternal course whether we are aware of it or not, whether we understand the cancer scourge or not, whether the human race exists or not. It does not seem to matter. One understands well the mood of the retired and praying monk who lives only to return to God. Knowing about the cosmic orgone ocean, one has a better understanding of and feeling for the essentially ascetic nature of all major religious systems. Nothing matters.[3]

In 1928, Jung received a translation of the alchemical Taoist text *The Secret of the Golden Flower* from his friend Richard Wilhelm, who asked him to write a foreword. Although Jung was not yet involved in alchemy, the manuscript was a great help to him in his education. Alchemy was a bridge for him to the early Gnostic traditions, whose symbology coincided with his observations of the collective unconscious, as revealed in the dreams of his clients. In an earlier time, when the study of the physical properties of matter was in its infancy, alchemy appeared to be a primitive forebear of modern chemistry. Earth, sulphur, mercury, salt, and other known substances were combined, heated, and distilled in conjunction with the alignment of the stars. Alchemy connected Jung with an ongoing mystical tradition. He found in this obscure byway a vast reserve of invaluable symbolic references that elucidated the psychic life of twentieth-century men and women. "Alchemy describes," he wrote, "not merely in general outline but often in the most astonishing detail, the same psychological phenomenology which can be observed in the analysis of unconscious processes."[4] In one of his client's dreams, for example, a flying eagle turned its head completely around and ate its own wings, an image representing a reversal in which one action creates its opposite. Jung found this same image in an alchemical work.[5]

Alchemy, for Jung, was not just a series of chemical experiments but dealt with "something resembling psychic processes expressed in pseudochemical language."[6] The alchemist was not after ordinary gold but the philosophical gold in the stone, the symbol of the irreducible self, "the incorruptible essence of man which would survive death, an essential part of the human being which could be preserved."[7] Since matter was a mystery to the medieval man, it served as a screen onto which he could project his unconscious experience. "The real nature of matter," wrote Jung, "was unknown to the alchemist: he knew it only in hints. In seeking to explore it he projected the unconscious into the darkness of matter in order to illuminate it."[8] Mercury, or quicksilver, was particularly fascinating, having properties of liquid and solid, properties that suggested miraculous change. Mercurius became for the alchemist the "world-creating spirit concealed or imprisoned in matter."[9] Like a mythic dragon, Mercurius devoured himself and died, only to be reborn as the philosopher's stone. Mercurius began and completed the alchemical work.

The alchemist prepared and heated material like earth and mercury in a retort, from which he expected to extract an essence, the spirit once trapped in matter; and through many distillations, he saw the breakdown of chaos into four elements: earth, fire, air, and water. The alchemist thought of creation as it is represented in *Genesis*, where, in the beginning, God moves upon the dark face of the waters. The squaring of the circle fascinated the medieval mind. As a symbol for the alchemical process, it represented the breaking down of the original chaotic unity into the four elements and their reordering into a higher unity.[10]

> The earth emerges from the chaotic waters of the beginning, from the *massa confusa*, in accordance with the ancient alchemical view; above it lies air, the volatile element rising from the earth. Highest of all comes fire as the "finest" substance, i.e., the fiery pneuma which reaches up to the seat of the gods.[11]

One might imagine looking into the heated retort and watching the steam ascend like a cloud on the mountain as the spiritual essences gather, only to condense as a distillate. The dark elements are lightened. In further alchemical processes, the sun and moon, male and female, hot sulphur and cool damp quicksilver, are brought to a divine marriage, the king and queen joined.

How odd, comments von Franz, that an object as common as a stone should be the goal of the alchemical work. "A stone," she notes, "neither eats nor drinks nor sleeps, it just remains there for all eternity."[12] The stone represents a kind of objective personality, a durable self that, out of suffering and confrontation with the unconscious, establishes itself as a neutral presence.[13] In researching the alchemical literature of the sixteenth and seventeenth centuries, Jung found a few practitioners who addressed the subjective personal nature of the work. In particular, Gerald Dorn was able to grasp the psychological implications of the work, insisting on the good character of the practitioners, who needed an ascetic attitude toward the world. Through the opus, the work, the alchemist first sought *unio mentalis*, which Jung understood to mean knowledge of oneself.

In the first stage, the attempt was to free the soul from its imprisonment in matter. Man is caught in his unawareness, his unconscious action, swept by the archetypal forces that play upon him, caught in the flesh of this world. The first stage for the practitioner is the facing of one's own darkness, the nigredo, the owning of one's shadow, whereby one is caught in a terrible depression and faces the "black raven," the devil. If the soul is to be freed, an engagement with Mercurius is necessary. Mercurius is the personification of the collective unconscious. Something outside our control must break through and engage us. The *Opus Alchymicum* describes the secret of creation, "which began with the incubation of the waters."[14] Mercurius, a living and universal spirit, descends to the earth to mix with impure sulphur and become entrapped. He can only be freed through the art of alchemy:

"But where is this golden Mercury, this radical moisture, which, dissolved in sulphur and salt, becomes the animated seed of the metals? Ah, he is incarcerated and held so fast that even nature cannot release him from the harsh prison, unless the master Art open the way."[15]

From the sun the light comes as a spirit of wisdom and teaches man the art whereby the "soul enchained in the elements" is freed. Mercurius, although a spirit of light, is a compound of opposites and contains as well the dark side, the subterranean Hermes, the snake, who ascends and descends, a *uroboros* (a circular symbol of a snake or dragon swallowing its own tail) that begets itself from itself. In darkness it lives on as the snake.[16]

Mercurius, it is generally affirmed, is the *arcanum*, the *prima materia*, the "father of all metals," the primeval chaos, the earth of paradise, the "material upon which nature worked a little, but nevertheless left imperfect." He is also the *ultimo materia*, the goal of his

151

own transformation, the stone, the tincture, the philosophic gold, the carbuncle, the philosophic man, the second Adam, the analogue of Christ the king, the light of lights, the *deus terrestris*, indeed the divinity itself or its perfect counterpart. . . . Mercurius is also the process which lies between, and the means by which it is effected. He is the "beginning, middle, and end of the work." Therefore he is called the Mediator, *Servator*, and *Salvator*. He is a mediator like Hermes.[17]

Jung felt that to engage Mercurius, the unconscious, one should take hold of him in some way, through active imagination. In the process of active imagination, one takes some product of the unconscious and confronts it:

Take the unconscious in one of its handiest forms, say a spontaneous fantasy, a dream, an irrational mood, an affect, or something of the kind, and operate with it. Give it your special attention, concentrate on it, and observe its alterations objectively. Spare no effort to devote yourself to this task, follow the subsequent transformations of the spontaneous fantasy attentively and carefully. Above all, don't let anything from outside, that does not belong, get into it, for the fantasy-image has "everything it needs." In this way one is certain of not interfering by conscious caprice, and of giving the unconscious a free hand. In short, the alchemical operation seems to us the equivalent of the psychological process of active imagination.[18]

The search for the *unio mentalis*, knowledge of oneself, at first plunges one into the nigredo, the dark night of the soul. But if the soul is to separate itself from the fetters of the world trap, then it must own its own projections and must engage the dragon and risk death or psychosis. The engagement with the dark ground of the self brings about a new centering in the self, less confined and with more than a mere ego orientation. The practitioner has also gained a self-reliance and sense of trust, an inner certainty. The emergence of this wholeness can be traced in the spontaneous expression of mandalas, of images, that unite out of the unconscious.

While the philosopher's stone or psychic wholeness seems difficult enough, a few alchemists saw a stage beyond, which was called *unus mundus*. *Unus Mundus* was the highest degree of conjunction, representing the union of the whole man with the *unus mundus*—"the potential world of the first day of creation, when nothing was yet 'in actu,' i.e., divided into two and many, but still one."[19] And this potential world is "the eternal ground of all empirical being, just as the self is the ground and origin of the individual personality, past, present, and future."[20] The work of alchemy was to bring about the union of opposites and to establish a state of being freed from the opposites, as in the Eastern concept of Atman and Tao. The third stage unites the adept with the *unus mundus*, psychologically understood as a synthesis of the conscious with the unconscious.

Reich had no alchemical intention when he began the work that led to the discovery of orgone. Nevertheless, he had a psychological framework that made him strangely similar to the medieval alchemists, who mostly had no subjective concepts of psyche. Just as they were able to project into the mystery of matter, Reich was full of wonder in his investigation of the birth of life from inanimate matter. He was finally in the laboratory, away from patients, with all the equipment he needed. Oslo was a paradise of opportunity for him. The use of high magnification for microscope work offered another way in which he could go out of focus and begin to establish more contact with his fourth function, intuition, the doorway to his unconscious. Reich changed after the mid-1930s. He had passed the midpoint of life, and other energies and concerns began to take place. In the second half of life, man turns inward and begins to develop in those areas hitherto ignored and undeveloped, according to Jung's theory of types of the eight possible modes of functioning. Both Jung and Reich began their serious work with alchemy and orgone, respectively, in the latter part of the 1930s.

In describing Reich's work as paralleling the alchemical process, I in no way wish to detract from his scientific work or to imply that his work was unscientific or "mystical" and that he merely deceived himself. As a nonscientist, I do not feel qualified to evaluate his scientific work. His hasty dismissal from orthodox science is another example of the persecution of the alchemist. The church hierarchy of American science, in collusion with the State,

found it necessary to burn his books. Hopefully, someone will ultimately establish his work or document the errors of his ways. At
least his work should be given a decent scientific funeral, instead
of leaving the remains for vultures and hyenas.

Reich sought to study vegetative currents microscopically in
protozoa. To prepare the protozoa, he was directed by the laboratory assistant at the Botanical Institute in Oslo, following standard procedure, to put hay and water together and to check them
after ten to fourteen days.[21] When he asked how the animals
entered the infusion of water and hay, he was reminded of the
germ theory. But in studying the grass in water continuously by
microscope, Reich became convinced that grass tissue was transformed through a transitional stage of developmental phases into
animal life, even though his observations clashed with the germ
theory. In order to prevent organisms from infiltrating his
preparations as germs in the air, he boiled the preparations for
fifteen to thirty minutes in closed glass containers. To his surprise,
*"the boiled preparations immediately exhibited newer and more active
forms of life than did the unboiled preparations after days of
swelling."*[22]

When Reich boiled earth in containers with potassium chlo-
ride and gelatin, the preliminary stages of life, the pseudo-amoe-
bae, exhibited movement that was slow and tremulous without any
inner flow—that is, "mechanical." Reich called these life-forms
"bions." To encourage the transition to animal life, he added leu-
trium, cholesterum, and egg white:

> Leutrium with potassium chloride alone does not produce cells, but
> only regularly formed tubes of various kinds. There is also no
> organic movement, but merely a growing and sprouting, apparently
> caused by the intake of fluid. Egg white to which only KCl
> [potassium chloride] is added does not result in any cell formation.
> However, egg white plus leutrium plus KCl plus cholesterum gives
> rise to cell formation.[23]

In further work, Reich added meat broth, milk, and egg yolk
as nutrients to the bion mixture, and carbon in various forms like
coal dust and soot heated to incandescence. He soon became convinced that life was created from inorganic matter.

It is hard to imagine modern scientists boiling earth in closed containers and adding salt. Such an image seems more suitable for an alchemist of the seventeenth century. The alchemists did not think psychologically, by and large, about their endeavors, but were fascinated by the mystery of matter and were able to project onto it the unconscious process triggered and stimulated by their genuine efforts and wonder. Reich also was able in a similar way to project his unconscious onto the scientific endeavor. By studying motion microscopically and then in the sky, he came upon a sense of connectedness and meaning in nature, and perhaps his years in the laboratory assisted the inner alchemy of his nature.

The most dramatic leap from his refutation of germ theory to his postulation of the presence of a pervasive life energy was initiated by a laboratory error:

> In January 1939, one of my assistants was demonstrating the incandescence experiment to a visitor in the laboratory in Oslo. By mistake, she took the wrong container from the sterilizer and instead of earth she heated ocean sand to incandescence. After two days a culture had started to form in the bouillon potassium chloride solution which, when innoculated on egg medium and agar, yielded a yellow growth. Under the microscope this new kind of culture appeared as large, scarcely motile, pockets of energy glimmering with an intense blue. The culture was "pure," i.e., it consisted of only *one* kind of formation. . . . These bions received the designation SAPA (*sand pa*cket). They possessed properties of extreme interest.
>
> The effect of the SAPA bions on rot bacteria, protozoa, and T-bacilli was much more powerful than that of other bions. Brought together with cancer cells, they killed or paralyzed the cells even at a distance of approximately 10 microns.[24]

Reich was aware of a radiation phenomenon that possessed unique properties. When tested for radiation by a radium physicist, the SAPA bions under a radium electroscope gave no reaction, and yet the SAPA bions in a tube held against the skin could redden the skin within a few minutes. The study of SAPA bions also produced conjunctivitis in both of Reich's eyes.

The room where the SAPA bions were kept needed constant ventilation, with the window open, or else workers suffered headaches. The air became "heavy," and metal objects became highly magnetic. Experimenting with photographic plates, Reich found that even the control plates in the room without the culture became fogged like the others, as if the energy were present everywhere.

Reich transferred his cultures to a dark basement, where, once his eyes adapted to the darkness, he saw the room not as black but as a grayish blue: "I saw fog-like vapors, streaks of blue light, and dots darting about. Light of a deep violet color seemed to come from the walls and the objects around the room."[25] After two hours, Reich was able to see "quite distinctly a radiation from the palm of my hand, the sleeves of my shirt, and (looking in the mirror) the hair on my head. Gradually, the blue glimmer surrounded my body and objects in the room like a hazy, slow-moving, gray-blue luminous vapor."[26] Reich found the radiation very irritating to the optic nerve; and others around him, exposed to the same phenomenon, saw much of what he saw. A businessman exposed to Reich's work commented, "I feel as if I've been staring into the sun for a long time."[27]

Indeed, solar energy would explain a great deal of Reich's thought: the "irritation of the eyes, the conjunctivitis, the rapid reddening of the skin, and its subsequent tanning. (I had conducted the experiments during the winter and early spring of 1939, had not been exposed to the sun, yet had a deep tan over my entire body.) I felt extremely vigorous, as 'strong as a bear,' and vegetatively alive in every respect."[28] Reich's fear at being exposed to a dangerous radiation eased, and he relaxed his protective measures. He was impressed that he had stumbled upon an energy with extremely high biological activity. What was the nature of this energy, and how was it to be measured?

> One day the idea "sun energy" suddenly occurred to me, providing a simple solution which sounded absurd only at first: *SAPA bions had originated from ocean sand. But ocean sand is nothing more than solidified solar energy. The incandescing and swelling of the sand had released this energy once again from its material state.*[29]

Reich also noticed that the cultures imparted an electric charge to rubber and other substances such as paper, cotton wool, and cellulose, which, from the absorbed energy, were able to cause the leaf on an electroscope to curl. "Humidity, shade combined with a strong breeze, or touching the substance with the hands for several minutes caused the effect to disappear."[30]

Reich called the energy orgone, since its discovery grew out of his work on the orgasm and because the energy was absorbed by organic matter. He decided to contain the radiation by building a box with metal on the inside to reflect and hold the radiation and with organic matter on the outside to reduce or prevent the transmitting of the radiation to the outside. With the culture placed inside the box, Reich "was able to distinctly observe blue moving vapors and bright, yellow-white streaks and dots of light. The phenomena were confirmed by several persons who served as subjects in repetitions of the experiment."[31] Reich was surprised when he saw the same phenomenon when the box was empty after having been thoroughly ventilated and cleaned. Other boxes constructed in the same manner produced the same visual effect.

In 1940, during a summer trip to Maine, Reich observed the flickering of stars and began to question the validity of the concept that the stars flickered because of the diffusion of light. He looked at the sky through a wooden tube, and at last his understanding of orgone energy fell into place:

> I began to look at individual stars through a wooden tube, at one point unintentionally aiming the tube toward a deep-blue spot in the sky between the stars. I was amazed to see a lively flickering followed by flashes of fine rays of light in the circular field of the tube. The phenomenon gradually faded as I moved the tube in the direction of the moon, being the most intense in the darkest portions of the sky *between* the stars. It was the same fine flickering and flashing, with dots and streaks of light, that I had observed so often in my box. I inserted a magnifying glass in the tube to enlarge the rays. Suddenly my box lost its mystery. The phenomenon had become quite understandable: *the radiation in my culture-free box originated in the atmosphere. The atmosphere contains an energy of which I had no previous knowledge.*[32]

In Reich, then, we find strong parallels with the alchemists, who heated the earth in closed retorts, who used salt, and who studied nigredo or decomposition and dissolution. Reich came to see that what men had once called ether, which fills all space and exists universally, was the all-pervading, observable, and demonstrable energy he called orgone. The alchemists also knew of the blue ether, the *lapis aetherius*, the Philosopher's Stone, considered to be the same phenomenon. In one of his most powerful passages in *The Murder of Christ*, Reich saw man in a trap. "The trap is man's emotional structure, his character structure,"[33] which man is born into and inherits from the culture. Alchemy also saw the world of matter as a trap. Mercurius entrapped in the world of impure sulphur can be released by the power of the sun, by SAPA bions, and by the soul released from the material prison through alchemical art. Reich, with his sense of connection to nature, certainly had glimpses of the *unus mundus*. His knowledge of himself, however, the *unio mentalis*, remained flawed.

Some people may object that I describe Reich as coming into a spiritual orientation when for so many years he was atheistic, and they may prefer to dismiss his last ten years as primarily the product of his emotional breakdown. But Reich himself acknowledged how schizophrenics penetrate to the core of life more easily than many neurotic, armored people. Even if we declare (as I do not) that he was "crazy" in his last years, we still need not dismiss the pungent insights and visions of life that he so beautifully expressed. To call Reich spiritual when most of his life was spent in opposition to a life-negating mysticism might contradict a basic tenet of his thought. But Reich himself was in the business of reminding people that their bodies express unconscious feelings and images that contradict their rational presentation of themselves. So it was with Reich himself. His blind spot was in the area of his own fervent intuition and movement to a spiritual framework, which he could partially acknowledge in his last years.

It is possible that, in time, we will discover that alchemy was indeed a symbolic process that transformed the inner heart of man, but also that alchemy put us in touch with the blue ether, the energy of the universe. We may also discover that Wilhelm Reich, as he claimed, confirmed through scientific means the reality of the blue ether, calling it orgone.

Notes

1. Marie-Louise von Franz, *Alchemy: An Introduction to the Symbolism and the Psychology*, ed. Daryl Sharp (Toronto: Inner City Books, 1980), pp. 37–38. This book is based on a series of lectures given by von Franz in 1959 at the C. G. Jung Institute in Zurich.

2. C. G. Jung, *The Archetypes and the Collective Unconscious*, trans. R. F. C. Hull, ed. Sir Herbert Read, Michael Fordham, and Gerhard Adler, Bollingen Series XX, vol. 9 (Princeton: Princeton University Press, 1980), pp. 129–130.

3. Wilhelm Reich, *Cosmic Superimposition*, trans. Mary Boyd Higgins and Therese Pol (New York: Farrar, Straus & Giroux, 1973), p. 278.

4. C. G. Jung, *The Psychology of the Transference*, Bollingen Series XX, vol. 16 (Princeton: Princeton University Press, 1974), p. 34.

5. Von Franz, *Alchemy*, p. 14.

6. C. G. Jung, *Psychology and Alchemy*, Bollingen Series XX, vol. 12 (Princeton: Princeton University Press, 1977), p. 242.

7. Von Franz, *Alchemy*, p. 93.

8. Jung, *Psychology and Alchemy*, p. 244.

9. Ibid., p. 293.

10. Ibid., p. 124.

11. Ibid., p. 264.

12. Von Franz, *Alchemy*, p. 169.

13. Ibid.

14. C. G. Jung, *Mysterium Coniunctionis: An Inquiry into the Separation and Synthesis of Psychic Opposites in Alchemy*, 2nd ed., trans. R. F. C. Hull, Bollingen Series XX, vol. 14 (Princeton: Princeton University Press, 1977), p. 339.

15. Ibid. Jung is quoting here from the *Opus Alchymicum*.

16. Ibid., p. 340.

17. C. G. Jung, *Alchemical Studies*, trans. R. F. C. Hull, Bollingen Series XX, vol. 13 (Princeton: Princeton University Press, 1967), p. 235.

18. Jung, *Mysterium Coniunctionis*, p. 526.

19. Ibid., p. 534.

20. Ibid.

21. Wilhelm Reich, *The Bion Experiments on the Origin of Life*, trans. Derek and Inge Jordan, ed. Mary Higgins and Chester M. Raphael (New York: Octagon, 1979), p. 25.

22. Ibid., p. 49 (italics in the original).

23. Ibid., p. 59.

24. Wilhelm Reich, *The Cancer Biopathy* [vol. 2 of *The Discovery of the Orgone*], trans. Andrew White with Mary Higgins and Chester M. Raphael (New York: Farrar, Straus, & Giroux, 1973), p. 82.

25. Ibid., p. 85.

26. Ibid., p. 86.

27. Ibid.

28. Ibid., p. 87.

29. Ibid., p. 86 (italics in the original).

30. Ibid., p. 88.

31. Ibid., p. 91.

32. Ibid., p. 94 (italics in the original).

33. Wilhelm Reich, *The Murder of Christ* [vol. 1 of *The Emotional Plague of Mankind*] (New York: Simon & Schuster, 1953), p. 3.

Chapter 12

Three Myths

What should we be without the sexual myth,
the human reverie or poem of death?

Castratos of moon-mask—life consists
of propositions about life. The human

Reverie is a solitude in which
we compose these propositions, torn by dreams,

By the terrible incantations of defeats
And by the fear that defeats and dreams are one.

The whole race is a poet that writes down
the eccentric propositions of its fate.

—Wallace Stevens, "Men Made Out of Words"

Freud, Jung, and Reich all became identified with a great drama that in some way identified them in their particular individuality.

Freud, after his self-analysis in 1897, established Oedipus as the central human drama, which he pronounced as universal, describing the child-parent condition on the level of secret wishes. He was known to have called his daughter Anna "Antigone," which was the name of Oedipus's daughter.

Like Freud, Oedipus initially feels betrayed and threatened by someone he trusts entirely, eventually becoming paranoid. Creon, his brother-in-law with whom he shares power equally, in all innocence sends the seer Tiresias to Oedipus, hoping that the blind man will have some explanation for the plague that has descended upon Thebes. Oedipus interprets the terrible words of Tiresias as part of Creon's plot to overthrow him.

Freud felt betrayed by Wilhelm Fliess, his closest friend until 1900. Later, this betrayal continued with the defections of Adler, Jung, and Rank. While these schisms were initially seen by Freud as attempts at overthrows, the Oedipal drama suggests that they were accompanied by a profound sense of guilt concerning an undisclosed involvement on Freud's part. "Ill-fated man," cries Jocasta, Oedipus's wife and mother. "May you never find out who you are!"

With enormous courage, Freud relentlessly sought out the truth of who he was. But from his early fifties on, he was resigned, bitter, even biting—a fact that both Jung and Reich commented on.[1] Oedipus is bitter as well, cursing the slave who allowed him to live as a baby, and blaming Apollo for fulfilling his fate: "But I am hateful to the gods above all men." Oedipus puts out his own eyes because nothing he can see will bring him joy. Oedipus does not die but continues life in pain, partially cut off from contact with the world. Similarly, Freud, who once spoke so beautifully, suffered from cancer of the jaw in 1923, after which, for several years, he was unable to speak at meetings. For the rest of his life, he was often in considerable pain. Concerning Freud's cancer, Reich said in an interview:

> He couldn't speak. You see, he had been a marvelous speaker. His words flew clearly, simply, logically. I remember that Berlin Congress. He was beautiful. He spoke about *Das Ich und das Es* [The Ego and the Id]. He spoke very clearly. And then it hit him right there in the speech organ.[2]

Our destiny appears to be our propensity, consciously or unconsciously, to live out a story with which we have identified.

Jung, the son of a minister in a family of ministers, felt no transcendental upliftment at his first communion, nor in the months to follow did he experience the grace that he expected to flow from the heart of Christ. His mother, reacting to his devastating despondency, handed him Goethe's *Faust,* and this became his myth.

In a purposeful parallel to the beginning of the story of Job, Goethe's God and Satan appear to be on good terms. Satan's task is to test the faithfulness of the flock, to exercise a more cynical, ironic view of life, while God, from lofty heights, expresses a benign contentment in the loyalty of his best subjects. While the most awful afflictions are visited upon Job for no apparent reason, in *Faust* Mephistopheles enters only at Faust's request.

The divine music that Faust hears cannot touch his heart. Faust is deeply accomplished, but unlike his apprentice, Wagner, he no longer finds solace or answers in dusty books. Faust accompanies his father, ministering to the plague victims, and is acclaimed as a healer, but he feels guilt and a sense of fraudulence.

His father, something of an alchemist, feeds his patients strange medicines, which Faust feels are more instrumental than the plague in their deaths. Beneath the veneer of fame and approval lies a dark side as yet unexplored. Jung, like Faust, felt a deep pain and disappointment with his father, and shared with him a loss of faith. His father, who represented the church, was unable to deal openly with his lack of inner ground.

But Jung, like Faust, sought through his dialogue with Mephistopheles to awaken the joy of life, for Mephistopheles holds the keys to the lower realms. Like Mercurius, he knows of the spirit caught in nature and can unleash the dark chthonic god of youth and sexuality. Faust's father, who has not integrated the dark side, is unable to ground his son, but Mephistopheles can, and Faust needs that grounding to progress. Faust suffers a mid-life crisis (as did Jung), and in that process he regains his youth and pursues his sexual interests in a second adolescence. Faust probably missed his adolescence through his obedient service to his father. Having initially experienced his depression, the nigredo, he pursues self-knowledge through a dialogue with the dark side.

After engaging the shadow, Faust meets the elusive, nourishing anima in the form of Gretchen, an innocent, beautiful, and reverent maiden. Faust acts worldly and openly schemes with Mephistopheles to seduce her. His involvement with her ultimately brings him release through her purity and faith, but causes her downfall and disgrace in a society that values virginity in women over every other virtue. Jung, like Faust, had to learn the ethical and appropriate use of his power and worldly knowledge in his relationships with women.

Jung's anguish and inner discrepancies plunged him into the dark night of the soul. He emerged in a better relationship to the feminine within himself and, presumably, was able to acknowledge and contain his projections.

Goethe was interested in alchemy, and therefore Jung was especially drawn to the second part of *Faust*, which he saw as the meeting with the collective unconscious. Faust obtains from Mephistopheles the key that allows him to descend to the deepest realms of the mothers, and his descent is an heroic trial. For Jung, then, *Faust* became a pattern that he followed consciously in his life and his theoretical work. Faust, a thinking type, finds through Mephistopheles a way to explore his fourth function, feeling, which leads into the deep levels of self.

Reich's drama was *Peer Gynt*. In October 1920, he wrote a paper on the subject, "Libidinal Conflicts and Delusions in Ibsen's *Peer Gynt*," which he presented to the Vienna Psychoanalytic Society.[3] When he rewrote *The Function of the Orgasm* in 1940, "Peer Gynt" was the title and subject of his second chapter:

> The world was in a state of transition and uncertainty at the time
> when I read and understood *Peer Gynt*, and when I met Freud and
> grasped his meaning. I felt an outsider, like Peer Gynt. His fate
> seemed to me the most likely outcome of an attempt to step out of
> line with official science and traditional thinking.[4]

Peer is a disruptive, unproductive youth. His father, once rich and respected, becomes an alcoholic, leaving the mother and son poor, embittered, and open to ridicule. Peer has a teasing, manipulative relationship with his mother, who dotes on him. Without a father, Peer is ungrounded in the world. He wanders for days in the woods, a great dreamer, an outsider. The small-minded community, totally focused on mundane business concerns, is amused and scornful at Peer's lies and exaggerations.

Like Peer, Reich had a mother fixation. So often alone as a child, he also was abandoned to nature. His mother, like Peer's, was allied with her son against the cruel father. Also like Peer, Reich, once part of a well-to-do family, was thrust into poverty.

Feeling unrelated to the world, Peer has extravagant dreams. "I'll be a king, an emperor," he tells his mother. In his dirty, tattered clothes, he is painfully sensitive to the scorn and contempt with which he is treated. Peer goes to a wedding and meets a girl, Solveig, but he steals the bride and sleeps with her in the fountain, then callously abandons her, evidence of his ambivalence toward the mother. The country people are enraged and search for him in the hills with guns and sticks.

As an outlaw, Peer feels as strong as a bear, able to engage the world and progress inwardly. In the mountains, he sleeps with a troll woman, the daughter of the troll king, who through ancient custom has a double shape. Palaces look like rubbish piles, black like white, ugly like fair. The trolls try to make Peer one of them, but his human nature persists, and he does not enjoy living among animals, eating cows' cakes and oxen's mead. His future wife is a cow in her other shape. Commitment to this woman and to this life is an ugly, intolerable way to ground himself in the world, and so Peer escapes.

Peer has his internal struggles. He battles a voice that obstructs his way but does not physically strike him. Peer is eventually able to pass through because, as the voice says, "He was too strong, there were women behind him." With all the inner and outer struggles that Reich experienced, there were always women who supported and helped him, too.

As Peer builds himself a hut in the woods, he notices how his dreaminess interferes with his work, but his limited insight does not diminish his behavior. Solveig, the girl he met at the wedding, seeks him out, devoting her life to him, but his troll princess returns as an old hag, dragging his ugly child with her, promising to be always beside him, a dark parallel to his love for Solveig. At the point where Peer might commit himself to someone and experience deep trust and intimacy, he is visited by the intolerable consequences and limitations of his past actions. The dark side of the mother will not let him go. Peer once more escapes and builds a fortune as a slave trader in America.

Unable to relate to the small-minded ethics of ordinary people, he is an outlaw, like Faust, sometimes insensitive, unfeeling, amoral, psychopathic, whose only goal is the furtherance of himself, an extreme and empty individualism. No longer provincial,

Peer, again like Faust, becomes a citizen of the world. He wishes to gain enough money to become emperor of the world, but he loses it all.

The rest of Ibsen's play is a comment on Peer's efforts to be himself, which is to follow his true destiny. The selfishness and isolation of his efforts are explored as he becomes emperor in a lunatic asylum. Later, he returns to the mountains, pursued by various death figures. He unpeels an onion, a symbol of himself, and finds no core, no kernel, only layers. The Button Moulder appears with an order to melt him down because he has never become himself, despite his posturing to the contrary. The Devil has no place for him because even his evil is uncommitted. Finally, Peer is saved from death by Solveig, who has waited faithfully for him in the hut so many years.

"Tell me, then," he asks, "where was my real self, complete and true—the Peer who bore the stamp of God upon his brow?" Solveig says, "In my faith, in my hope, and in my love." Like Faust, Peer is finally saved by the devotion and purity of a woman—one who holds in her heart a sense of his true being that he cannot sustain by himself.

Like Peer, Reich was restless and seemingly unable to make an intimate commitment to a woman. Instead, women became instruments of his larger design as he was driven by his dreams of greatness. Like Peer, he remained unsettled, a citizen of the world, at war with provincialism, and yet in danger of remaining morally undeveloped, an exploiter of others. Faced with Peer's dilemma, Reich tried to resolve the issue of his egoistic isolation and ungroundedness in another way. When Reich unpeeled the onion of self, he found armoring and finally the core. Peer's Solveig, like Faust's Gretchen, represents the untouched childlike purity of inner soul, a level of feminine innocence that for Reich was the core. Like Peer, Reich had a spontaneous, restless energy, a youthful, childlike innocence and charm, an innate purity. He was a dreamer, a man of vision, a man of courage.

Reich was not altogether pleased with Peer the dreamer, whom he felt lacked sufficient force to make his place in the world. Reich felt that Brand, a rigid moralistic preacher in Ibsen's play of the same name, was a better model: "One has to be like Brand to achieve what Peer Gynt wants. But then, Brand does not have enough imagination. Brand has strength, but Peer Gynt feels life itself."[5]

Although Reich taught others to surrender, to let go, in his own life he was in conflict. Peer is finally able to surrender in the arms of Solveig and trust his identity to her loving heart, to let go of himself, and is in this way saved. Reich did not appear to give up his war with the world. He remained connected to nature and to innocence, but still an outlaw in the eyes of the world. Peer Gynt is an intuitive who does not know how to cooperate with the world. Reich's process was too rigidly focused, as if to stifle the intuitive life within.

All three dramas bring their protagonists into the life-and-death struggle to know who they are. Oedipus is bitter and injured; Faust is world-weary, callous, and enlightened; and Peer is grandiose, spontaneous, a dreamer who finds resolution in surrender to a simple loving woman. These dramas quite subtly delineate the uniqueness of Freud's, Jung's, and Reich's journeys in the world and tell us something of the myths that governed them.

Notes

1. In *Memories, Dreams, Reflections*, rev. ed., trans. Richard and Clara Winston, ed. Aniela Jaffé (New York: Pantheon, 1973), p. 152, Jung wrote: "There was one characteristic of [Freud's] that preoccupied me above all: his bitterness." Similarly, Reich wrote, in *Reich Speaks of Freud* (New York: Farrar, Straus & Giroux, 1967), pp. 20–21: "There is little doubt that [Freud] was very much dissatisfied genitally. Both his resignation and cancer were evidence of that. Freud had to give up, as a person. . . . He smoked very much, very much. I always had the feeling—not nervousness, not nervousness—but because he wanted to say something which never came over his lips . . . as if he had to 'bite something down.' . . . He was always very polite, 'bitingly' polite, sometimes."

2. Reich, *Reich Speaks of Freud*, p. 73.

3. Wilhelm Reich, "Libidinal Conflicts and Delusions in Ibsen's *Peer Gynt*," in *Wilhelm Reich: Early Writings*, trans. Philip Schmitz (New York: Farrar, Straus & Giroux, 1975), vol. 1, pp. 3–64.

4. Wilhelm Reich, *The Function of the Orgasm*, trans. Theodore P. Wolfe (New York: Meridian, 1970), p. 21.

5. Reich, *Function of the Orgasm*, p. 27.

Chapter 13

What Reich and Jung Could Have Learned from Each Other

I think I could turn and live with animals, they are
so placid and self-contain'd,
I stand and look at them long and long.
They do not sweat and whine about their condition,
they do not lie awake in the dark and weep for their sins,
they do not make me sick discussing their duty to God,
not one is dissatisfied, not one is demented with the
mania of owning things,
not one kneels to another, nor to his kind that lived
thousands of years ago
not one is respectable or unhappy over the whole earth.

—Walt Whitman, "Song of Myself"

Jung and Reich never met each other. Jung, a generation older, had abandoned the rigid tenets of psychoanalysis years before Reich as a young man joined Freud's group in the 1920s. To my knowledge, Jung never mentioned Reich; and Reich, until the 1950s, completely dismissed Jung's work without much elaboration. Nevertheless, in my fantasy I have wondered what Reich and Jung might have given each other had they sustained an association. Initially, I imagine a distant theoretical jockeying around, with laughter and sudden conflict, but, with time, the deeper levels they held in common would emerge with mutual surprise—and comfort. As remarkable therapists, they resorted to self-analysis, unable to find adequate therapists for themselves. In my fantasy of them as therapists to each other, I have pictured Jung saving Reich from his unsuccessful struggles with the world, and I have seen Reich breaking through the sophisticated walls of distrust that protected Jung from a more intimate contact with men.

Jung was far more cautious, more hidden, less exposed in the world. In sheer mental capacity, he was certainly one of the most brilliant psychologists of his time. Furthermore, he had a driving constitution that supported him in the most obscure byways of scholarship. Reich, on the other hand, was a man of enormous energy and a single-minded compulsive focus, little humor, and little interplay of metaphor. And yet it was his very singleness of focus that led into the heart, into the core of man. He insisted that people be present, be in contact, and he interrupted every defense that prevented the emergence of the spontaneous life within.

But in my speculation I have wanted to save Reich from his rigid intellectual framework, for he outran his vocabulary. He was more at home in biological terminology than expansive psychological metaphors. Nevertheless, his experiences went far beyond even psychological language, which he ultimately abandoned in favor of what he conceived to be science. Not that I join others to discredit his science. Rather, I would have had him look from another perspective at his work. His "functionalism" acknowledged that the old physics was dead. Nature was no longer out there to be studied objectively, but the observer and the observed were interconnected. The new physics of relativity and quantum theory has expressed man's relationship to the world in mathematical eloquence, but Reich had hold of only an insufficient piece of that truth. The community of modern science has the efficient beauty of counteracting the egocentricity of its members by rigorous demands of validation. Reich was isolated from others and, like Ibsen's Peer Gynt, self-taught. Without mutual interaction, the pace of modern science is such that to be out of touch with the work of others is to promote the likelihood of duplication. Reich took his example from Freud, the great man, the lonely thinker and pioneer, an older model for science when the pace was more benign.

I have found that some writers do not like Reich. Colin Wilson, for example, was disappointed to find in Reich the kind of man who was rigid and needed to be right. A colleague of mine, after reading what I had written about Reich in the manuscript for this book, concluded that she much preferred Jung. "But can't you see," I blurted out, "what lies behind the abruptness of his personality?" I think of personality as the clothes we manage to throw on in a panic as we abandon the ship of our childhood. Reich, so very sensitive within, needed his aggression to survive the early, tragic deaths of his parents. He needed protection amid the sly, indirect, political cattiness of the Viennese psychoanalytic group. At least he was courageous; he took chances. He exposed himself and was bold. He gave to the world. He had a large heart barely kept covered by his ambition, his driving sense of destiny. So I have loved Reich as a person and only felt pain and regret that he sabotaged his own happier future.

He was a great and moving teacher. During the social unrest of the late 1920s, disseminating sexual information as a Socialist, he went out into the streets and worked with the poor, having known something of poverty himself. Because of his heart and his charm, he was able to reach hundreds of people and educate them about their bodies and about freedom, which he did at his own expense. If he was so utterly rigid and self-righteous, how could he have learned about surrender and defended a true sexual embrace? Why would Freud have accepted and defended Reich before his jealous accusers unless Reich's brilliance had impressed him? As late as 1928, in a letter to Lou Andreas-Salomé, Freud was still mentioning Reich with respect, although challenging his youthful oversimplifications:

> We have here a Dr. Reich, a worthy but impetuous young man, passionately devoted to his hobby-horse, who now salutes in the genital orgasm the antidote to every neurosis. Perhaps he might learn from your analysis of K. to feel some respect for the complicated nature of the psyche.[1]

Unlike Jung, Reich was never able to win a protected life for himself, not even finally in Rangely, Maine. I think of William Blake's "Proverbs of Hell" in regard to Reich: "The fox provides for himself, but God provides for the lion."[2] I have a special regard for the diamond in the rough. I know the faults are on the outside where I can see them, and there are no deeper ugly surprises. My wish for Reich, then, was a therapy that would ease his tension with the world without destroying the force he needed to be heard. He was afraid that he would end up a mere dreamer like Peer Gynt unless he worked incessantly. I am convinced that an inward alchemy took place that brought Reich to a very high level of spiritual understanding.

Reich unconsciously knew how to isolate himself, and he had an instinct for the shadow in each situation. He called up in each group the very issues they refused to face. In Vienna, the analysts of the 1920s were finally successful, innovative, and protected from the social unrest around them; they were, in short, an elite club. Individually, on a professional level, Reich pointed out technical deficits in psychoanalytic practice, and politically he realigned with socialism. As a Socialist, he attacked the Communist party leadership for remaining safely distant from riots, and he disturbed their unconscious bourgeois predispositions through his explicit sexual education of the youth. He was drawn to the left-handed way, to taking an instinctive plunge into the dark side of life. Being drawn to the shadow, Reich was able to intuit latent resistance in his patients, but his disturbing unconscious gift disrupted stable social relationships. Jung's theoretical awareness of the shadow might have been useful to Reich in protecting himself, assuming that he were able to incorporate such knowledge and attend more carefully to his own process.

Reich's concept of character, as developed and complex as it was, was not sufficiently inclusive. He needed to ask the question that Jung had asked of himself during his stormy years of self-discovery in 1912–1917: "What myth am I living?" For Reich surely was governed by myth. His myth was initially taken from Freud, who saw himself as a brave pioneer in the face of a resistant world, one of a band of scientific fighters who used reason as a sword against the darkness of unconscious images. Reich shared with Freud an image of isolated greatness, a sense of being remembered historically, of having his life documented, of people later seeing that he was right after all, a kind of Darwin of the twentieth century, the scientific discoverer of life. From his naive unconscious acceptance of his myth, Reich seemed a child, a Peer Gynt.

Jung had dealt with the myth that governed him. He searched it out and took possession of it, and, while he understood the rages of ego around reputation and fame, he kept himself private. Jung attended Vanity Fair and did not purchase anything, but removed himself, gave himself distance, and lived as one who was a part of more than his own century. As a young man, Jung had made enemies and protected himself, paraded his strength, and bullied his opponents; but in his later years, he told one young admirer: "I am nothing; I am an old man. I no longer lie. Once, perhaps, I had to, as a young scientist without a reputation. Now I no longer lie."[3] He gave up on the world after his breakup with Freud and the psychic collapse that ensued after 1913. Jung would never again engage the world so directly. He hid away and spent months predominantly alone, initially at his home in Kusnacht and later in his turreted retreat at Bollingen, writing and thinking. In his late thirties, Jung withdrew from the world and was supported, even in his introversion, by peacefulness and a successful practice. Reich attempted to find his retreat in Rangely, Maine, toward the end of his life, when he was harassed and goaded by the outside world. His peace was severely interrupted.

And so, in my fantasy, Reich and Jung would have talked together about relating to the world, about being famous and recognized as Reich never really was. He was controversial, he was appreciated by a few followers, but he was never showered with recognition as were Freud and Jung. No universities gave Reich honorary degrees, nor did they ask him to speak. Freud and Jung knew how to be great men and get what they needed from their environment, but Reich was unable to build much for himself before he found it necessary to tumble it down. Perhaps it was his driven creative process, but had he been pushed into observing his myth, he might have rewritten his life. His final myth of the crucified Christ was played out in the most painful way. Legal advisers could easily have saved him from prison, but Reich was driven on by the Christ myth.

Jung knew the danger of identifying with an archetype. When the "wise old man" is acted out in us, when the great prophet voice arises in us, we are only an instrument. Nietzsche had identified his ego with Zarathustra, the prophetic voice that had possessed him. Identification with an archetype inflates the ego

173

and eventually threatens us with severe psychic imbalance. Unfortunately, Reich did not have the vocabulary in his system to deal with such phenomena. He suffered from ego identification with the archetype of the great man. At times, in his writing, he postured, displaying a penchant for self-important new catchwords. And yet there is a naive, childlike quality in this, a way in which he tried to buck himself up with self-applause because of his isolation. There is even in Reich's foolishness a great and touching vulnerability, because he truly was a great man and spirit. Believing in the power of therapeutic intervention, I fantasize Reich's confusion magically cleared away. Many people are destroyed by suffering, and a few are ennobled, inwardly raised up and clarified. Reich's identification with Jesus had some justification.

Reich was quite paranoid at times in the 1950s, after the assaults he had received over half a century of life. Perhaps he still kept locked in his heart the conviction that he had killed his mother and therefore was doomed like Cain to wander homeless upon the face of the earth, unable to enjoy the warmth and intimacy of friends. It is quite touching to read that during his last years, when planes flew overhead, Reich felt that the Air Force was looking after him. He could be very concrete. In the 1930s, in order to see energetic flow in life, he raised the optics of his microscope to an astonishing degree—the perfect way for Reich the scientist to go out of focus and push his awareness into a more intuitive seeing. Unable to adopt a spiritual vocabulary to explore and express his need for protection, he could count on the Air Force to provide him with that sense of semi-divine caring.

Jung claimed that the unconscious psyche holds images of god, which it projects out most easily onto whatever the conscious mind fails to understand. The awareness of projection is at the heart of Eastern religious disciplines, and Jung placed this awareness at the heart of his psychological work. But Reich, still holding desperately with childlike necessity to the concreteness of the world, felt reassured by the airplanes.

In his last days, tragically, after years of brilliant discovery, Reich built extensive sequence of delusions around flying saucers. In *A Book of Dreams*, Peter Reich, his son, vividly portrays Reich's sense of involvement with extraterrestrial life.[4] Jung, on the other hand, felt that the sightings of saucers were projections of the self by the unconscious. The large magical discs from another planet concretized the circle, the symbol of wholeness that people yearn for and project out onto the world. Only in later writings did he begin to allow for the possibility of their reality outside an unconscious projection. Reich, who saw flying saucers with his own eyes, might have profited from Jung's observations; and Jung might have profited from Reich's indefatigable attention to the outside world.

Reich would also have profited from Jung introducing him to Taoism and other Eastern modes of thought, in which sexuality and spirituality are powerfully interwoven and the spiritual is not divorced from the body. He would have learned new languages regarding spiritual realities, an Eastern scientific matter-of-factness. By the 1950s, Reich's emergence into the spiritual arena was blatant, but always guarded and militant, as if he were conquering new territory. He was an explorer for science very much the way the white man took over the west: self-righteously, as though the Indians were ignorant and had no real culture or awareness. Although Reich said that everyone is right in some way, he was not always able to tolerate the views of others.

Jung exercised more social charm. He was able to understand others' views intellectually. But there is no real evidence that he felt comfortable with competitors, either. He surrounded himself predominantly with women; the men he sent away to test their strength in the world. Politically, Jung was far more sophisticated than Reich. He knew how to outmaneuver, withdraw, overpower. Reich might have been consoled by Jung's wisdom in dealing with the world. Reich might also have envied the financial freedom that allowed Jung to withdraw when he chose.

Ideally, Jung would have broken through Reich's ego inflation and armoring, but Jung would also have profited from therapy with Reich. Feeling was Jung's inferior function, his blind side, and unexpressed feeling lay trapped in his body as chronic tension. If Reich was literal, provincial, concrete, and rigid in his approach, he was also extremely vulnerable, personable, and present in his heart. Jung, enormously charming, continuously isolated by the transference that people placed on him, so much the image to others of the Magician, the wise old man, was accustomed all his life to living alone. Reich, a brilliant therapist, would have challenged the charming, cool glint in Jung's eye and had him come clean. Reich would have helped Jung to express his rage and disappointment, and his posture of controlled distance would have been shaken. Jung was probably not as conscious of his irritation and powerful rage as he might have been. In his old age, it periodically broke out of him, and he had to beg the forgiveness and indulgence of his housekeeper. A kind of warring spirit in him uncaged itself from time to time as he lost his grip after an illness. It made its appearance in *The Answer to Job*, not so much in the content as in a surly, rough, sarcastic tone that flared up in the prose.

Reich would have challenged, as no one else dared, Jung's definitive structure for keeping distance and controlling contact, and then on a body level he would have seen Jung soften. Jung's paranoia and injury might have surfaced. Jung's heart, so passionate and yet guarded, would have come far more into the open. He would have shared more with others and felt more at ease in company. Perhaps his dependence on women would have occupied a few therapeutic hours, his projected anima finding a new level of integration, even though Jung worked for years on the anima issue. Through vegetotherapy, Reich would have assisted Jung toward a greater openness of heart and body. Threads of an unresolved homosexual fear, fleetingly mentioned in his letters to Freud, would have found more room to unwind. And finally, having been the father to so many others, Jung would have allowed himself to be fathered, something never resolved with his own father or with Freud.

Jung had some letting go to do, some collapsing. He needed, on a body level, to learn how to surrender. Always the powerful teacher, among his devotees he was not able to escape the transferences placed upon him. Jung had held himself together for years against the fear of becoming psychotic; even after his confrontation with the unconscious, he still wondered what would happen if he let down his guard. He went to Africa in the 1920s, not only as a scientist to study primitive people, but also to seek the answer to the question "What is going to happen to Jung the psychologist in the wilds of Africa?" He left Africa shortly after having a dream that warned him that the primitive man within had awakened and threatened to take over. According to Jung's writings, the archaic or primitive man in each of us has been lost through developing civilization. The primitive man was vital, unintellectual, directly and emotionally involved, not distinguishing inner from outer phenomena, and hence lived in a magical, numinous world of nature in which he unquestioningly belonged. Reich would have helped Jung to evoke the latent primitive man within himself, still dangerous and threatening to the civilized ego, but manageable and dramatically expressive in body-oriented therapy. While physical and earthy by nature, Jung never found so direct a path to the primitive man. And this primitive bodily expression, with its wrenching, abandoned feeling, would, in the presence of a trusted male therapist, have released great healing.

Both Jung and Reich may have hoped that Freud would fulfill their longing for a caring and emotionally available father. In 1926, Reich was bitterly disappointed when Freud refused to analyze him. Jung had attempted earlier to heal the split with his father through his relationship with Freud. For weeks, Freud and Jung traveled together on their visit in 1909 to lecture at Clark University in the United States. Jung later dated his disaffection with Freud to this time. During their exchange of dreams, Freud personalized Jung's dreams, reducing their meaning in ways similar to the narrow, reductive belief system of Jung's father. When Jung demanded more background information about a dream that Freud had presented, Freud recoiled, apparently feeling that his authority would be jeopardized. The choice of authority over self-disclosure by the greatest exponent of truth and honesty of the twentieth century must have sent Jung reeling. Jung's father had held onto his authority by withholding. How could Jung continue to see Freud as the heroic father who included him and was worthy of his wholehearted allegiance?

Jung had wanted to heal his father's loss of faith, but the rigid, angry man would have none of it. With Jung and Freud, there was a chance for great men to talk to each other, to heal each other, to penetrate disguises in the name of truth and give up all defenses, to abandon caution and no longer fear for one's image in the world. And now, in my imagination, Jung has a chance once more to enter into a realm of truth with an equal. Who else was there for Reich to talk to about his crushing rejection by Einstein? After all, Jung had met Einstein and worked with Pauli. In 1941, when Einstein was at Princeton, Reich arranged a meeting with him. The great man seemed quite engaged with Reich's theory of orgone and was willing to test out his accumulator. In a later letter to Reich, Einstein explained away the difference in temperature in Reich's orgone accumulator in an unsatisfactory way and cut off further discussion. In a similar way, Freud had explained away psychic phenomena that Jung had demonstrated to him in March 1909. In Freud's library, Jung had felt a severe heat in his diaphragm. A moment later, Jung and Freud were startled by a sharp noise from the bookcase. Jung claimed it as an example of a "catalytic exteriorization phenomenon"; but Freud, in effect, said, "bosh." Jung somehow knew that the noise would be repeated, and correctly predicted another sound a moment later. Afterwards, in letters, Freud explained the experience away. It simply did not fit into his system of belief.

Jung would have drawn Reich inward, away from the outer wound of rejection by the world, led him away finally by showing Reich his forebears, his antecedents in the search for universal life energy. He would have told him alchemical truths, and Reich would have proclaimed that he could prove it all with a Geiger counter, measuring orgone and establishing once and forever the philosopher's stone. Jung would have shown Reich a huge stone cube that he carved in his garden, which came to him "by accident" while he was building his tower in Bollingen. The stone had been rejected by the builders as the cornerstone of the tower because it was the "wrong" size. Symbolically, both Jung and Reich would have identified with that stone, having themselves been rejected by the master builder of their own profession. Left adrift by the culture, both, like Christ, brought revelation and healing and were rejected. Their truths frightened others.

Perhaps, after shared analysis, Jung and Reich would have held seminars on the mind/body split in Western culture. They would have talked about Jesus and about Hermes. Jung saw the unnatural split in the development of Christianity between good and evil, between Christ and the Devil. Since the dark side of human nature cannot be driven out, it is driven underground. We need an integrating symbol for the darkness and light. Jesus, who took upon himself the dark side, the sins of the world, became a Church symbol and was elevated above the human condition. But Hermes, who was the messenger of the gods, a phallic figure friendly to man, was often in the shadows. Jung, through his rigid and fearful early Christian training, had difficulty in utilizing Jesus as a unifying symbol without assistance from Hermes. Reich, on the other hand, saw Jesus as very much of the earth, sexual, alive, innately healthy, a genital man free of armor, whose healing powers inevitably flowed from his healthy uncompromised being, free from the traps of the world and in touch with the energy of the universe. Jung and Reich would have spoken of the power of nonverbal techniques, of body therapy and symbols, of myths and character, of transference and UFOs, of Taoism, of the mass man and individuation, of the hope and futility of therapy, of the power of breath, the inner path, yoga, and the streaming of energy in the body and in the sky. They would have talked about the night sky.

And they would have talked of Vienna. Jung would nod appreciatively at Reich's insights into Freud's followers. Both Reich and Jung would talk of Freud's resignation and bitterness, which kept Freud from embracing them fully in their psychological beliefs. Jung attributed Freud's resignation to his inability to break through into a spiritual dimension; Reich, to his being hemmed in by his organization, a genital character unable to bite through and clarify his sexuality on a personal or theoretical level. So each projected onto Freud's resignation what was close to his own heart.

In my fantasy, a great bond would grow between Reich and Jung—an unlikely friendship, people would say, unexpected but touching. They would soften in each other's presence and defer to each other—qualities that would be clear evidence of successful character analysis and individuation. For they would find in each other their own strategies of isolation, and finally find ways to trust each other with each difficult truth without recourse to defensive authority. So many subjects would have stimulated them. So much could have been gained. Each man, so apparently bold in thought, often felt endangered in the presence of other great compelling minds. They needed the silence to feel out the fragile web of their own imaginings. How long could Reich and

Jung have remained friends? How long did Gauguin and Van Gogh work together? But the meetings might have produced extraordinary results. Who else is to be the therapist of a great therapist? We can only speculate that Jung would have found release in his heart and body, and Reich would have found more elbow room for his great soul.

Notes

1. Ernst Pfeiffer, ed., *Sigmund Freud and Lou Andreas-Salomé: Letters*, trans. William and Elaine Robson-Scott (New York: W. W. Norton, 1985), p. 174.

2. William Blake, *Poems and Letters*, ed. J. Bronowski (Middlesex, England: Penguin, 1986), p. 96.

3. Maud Oakes, *The Stone Speaks: The Memoir of a Personal Transformation* (Wilmette, Ill.: Chiron Publications, 1987), p. 15.

4. Peter Reich, *A Book of Dreams* (Greenwich, Ct.: Fawcett, 1973), pp. 17–31.

Chapter 14

The Body As More Than the Shadow

When primal dawn spread on the eastern sky
her fingers of pink light, Odysseus' true son
stood up, drew on his tunic and his mantle,
slung on a sword belt and a new-edged sword,
tied his smooth feet into good rawhide sandals,
and left his room, a god's brilliance upon him.
He found the criers with clarion voices and told them
to muster the unshorn Athenians in full assembly.
The call sang out, and the men came streaming in;
and when they filled the assembly ground, he entered,
spear in hand, with two quick hounds at heel;
Athena lavished on him a sunlit grace
that held the eye of the multitude. Old men
made way for him as he took his father's chair.

—Homer, *The Odyssey*, Book II

To talk of the body as more than the shadow is to relinquish the pessimism of the twentieth century and take heart, once more affirming the living being of man. A culture that has trafficked so in public images of flesh has also denigrated the individual, so we look at bodies, not people, in our magazines. Young flesh in all its primitive exuberance can hide, to untrained eyes, the lack of identity and internal organization. Like Disney's bear cubs, these images are always "cute," always the same, a piece of collective nature with no individual significance. Such rootless,

181

ungrounded life is seed that falls on shallow ground; it springs up quickly, but in the heat of midday withers away. The body as more than the shadow is not restricted to youth, but extends to those who have entered the inner journey and faced their shadow. The body at mid-life is profoundly capable of change, but it must be a change of internal images as well as a release of chronic muscular tension. At mid-life the body can contract swiftly into disease and death, or break open into a ripeness where inner and outer beauty are more closely aligned. With increasing age, the inner images must come forward and predominate.

If we need to be reminded of images of the body as more than the shadow, we might look to Michelangelo's David, which so powerfully represents being in the present. One also senses the numinous presence of life in much of ancient Greek sculpture, created before the psyche's divorce from the body had taken place. To see the unity we have lost, we may turn, like Rilke, to the animals we have caged, as if to drive them into our despair:

> From seeing the bars, his seeing is so exhausted
> that it no longer holds anything anymore.
> To him the world is bars, a hundred thousand
> bars, and behind the bars, nothing.
>
> The lithe swinging of that rhythmical easy stride
> which circles down to the tiniest hub
> is like a dance of energy around a point
> in which a great will stands stunned and numb.
>
> Only at times the curtain of the pupils rise
> without a sound . . . then a shape enters,
> slips through the tightened silence of the shoulders,
> reaches the heart, and dies.[1]

The body is not only shadow but light. The body that breaks down, that imposes its own set of limitations outside the considerations of the conscious mind, that apparently at random develops a tendency, a weakness, a disability, represents a total living self. The body sets the terms for how the spirit of man is shaped in the world, and its word appears to be final. The mind can rant against the injustice of a bad back, but its arguments have no relevance in the world, and the attempt of the mind to set itself apart from the body creates a fool's paradise, a world of unrealized dreams. A body uninformed by mind and spirit may be given over to instinctual life or callous imitations, but a mind uninformed by the body loses its judgment and, in unforeseen and critical ways, blunders and retreats. Without the body, the wisdom of the larger self cannot be known.

We abandon the body because we cannot tolerate the limitations imposed by character armor, its burdened, darkened aspect. As children we are trained into blindness and unnecessary fears, and we eat the poisons our parents eat, unawares. "If the doors of perception were cleansed," wrote Blake, "everything would appear to man as it is, infinite. For man has closed himself up, till he sees all things thro' narrow chinks of his cavern."[2] Like Reich, Blake saw the repressive force of the Church and State destroying sexual expression and closing down the body of joy. It is, he said, the "cunning of weak and tame minds which have the power to resist energy."[3] Blake drew the bodies of men and women in an exalted state as bodies of light, full of energy and power. It was Blake's view that the ancient poets had animated the world with gods and goddesses, attaching names to them and identifying them with woods and trees and rivers, and that, later, a system and priesthood developed that took advantage of ordinary people, assuming authority by presuming to speak for the gods. "Thus men forgot that all deities reside in the human breast."[4]

The body of light is seen in Christ's resurrection. He instructs Thomas, who doubts, to place his hands on the still fresh wounds, and the resurrected Christ eats and drinks with his disciples—no ghost, no apparition. In contradiction to the embodied Christ, Christianity, in its fight against paganism, placed a curse upon the flesh and drove the great hooved Pan of nature into seclusion as if he were the Devil. The body of man awakened briefly in the Renaissance, discovering the magic of Greek paganism, but fell off once again into an abstracted, detoured reverie. Reich came to feel that the damage to the body of man was irreversible. Only through the acceptance of sexuality throughout childhood and through a culture that preferred self-regulation and individual autonomy over passive behavior could a new body, spontaneous and alive, support an unpathological society. Once a piece of paper is folded, the crease cannot be ironed out; but while character may be set for life, the damage can be reversed. We can own our projections, we can loosen the constrictions in our chest and pelvis and feel the flood of life once more. We can directly engage the body in movements that relate to its shadow.

Alexander Lowen, the founder of Bioenergetics, extended past the confines of biological metaphor and attended to the idioms of language. Idiom is a natural expression of the breadth of the human psyche, and, as such, includes both sexual and spiritual longing. Around issues of religion, Lowen was cautious. Like Jung, he rightly did not want to become a metaphysician and split the psyche he sought to heal. As a therapist, one might encourage all deep expressions of longing, spiritual and sexual, without drawing conclusions for the client.

Not only did Lowen's attention to language liberate Bioenergetics, but posturally he got the body out of bed. Reich worked with people lying down; with Lowen, the vocabulary of man's movement expanded to the potentiality of the dancer. If in fact the body and mind are two sides of the same coin, the unrestricted movement of the body represents a dramatic release from psychological restriction and death. As a therapist, to work with the body lying down is more useful in the context of a full range of postures, including standing, reaching, stretching, bending, and hitting. Reich had developed the concepts of holding back, collapse, surrender, and the orgasm reflex. Lowen developed in the standing posture the concept of grounding, in which the standing body needs to feel the function and strength of the legs, supporting itself in the world. Lowen's postures developed a more flexible ego, able to integrate the regressive outpourings of the prone position. Lowen was able to find useful postures in Eastern disciplines and also used the Eastern concept of centering in the *hara* (belly).

If Reich, like Moses, led the chosen people into the desert, then Lowen brought them into the promised land, to the walls of Jericho, the self. Reich was the pioneer; Lowen's genius was as a technician, a brilliant strategist in the day-to-day therapeutic intervention. Lowen developed and codified the character definition that Reich had postulated, and he reduced to essential statements the different personality styles. While Lowen never flaunted a new philosophy of the body, he instinctively created a more permanent breadth of movement that evokes a trust, a hopefulness that the body is greater than the shadow, and inborn in his work is an American optimism for nature as an abundant healer.

Lowen grounded his five character types in Freud's developmental stages. In this way he built a foundation for a psychology of the body that relates to the wide range of twentieth-century psychology. While Lowen's work has brought Reich's name forward, Lowen was by no means a popularizer; rather, he was—and still is—a superb stylist with a taste for simplicity and unpretension. In the language of the body, Lowen has found the body as more than the shadow. He has worked to develop the body in harmony with itself, graceful and at ease.

For Jung, the so-called mystic, the greatest of mysteries were present in the body itself. From his studies of Eastern yogic practices, he knew of the production of the "diamond body," the development of something eternal and durable in the laboratory of one's life. And he knew that the alchemy he sought involved similar bodily changes. The creation of the philosopher's stone, a durable self in a world of change and decay, and even the formation of symbolic images from the unconscious, is reflected in the body. "The formation of symbols," Jung wrote, "is frequently associated with physical disorders of a psychic origin, which in some cases are felt as decidedly 'real.'"[5] He continued: "The symbols of the self arise in the depths of the body, and they express its materiality every bit as much as the structure of the perceiving consciousness. The symbol is thus a living body, *corpus et anima.*"[6]

The Eastern mind feels that thought itself has substance. Man as a living being, said Jung, outwardly appears as a material body, which inwardly manifests itself as "a series of images of the vital activities taking place within it. They are two sides of the same coin."[7] Rather than working directly on the body, Jung chose to work with the symbols, knowing that they had a materiality of their own, and profoundly shifted the energy of the body.

Symbols, Jung reasoned, either reflect the archaic physiology of the body or are more differentiated, reflecting the more conscious character. Within the human body reside the entire range of symbols from the most primitive to the most differentiated; thus, the symbol of the snake emerging in a fantasy or dream is directly connected to the body function:

More especially the threat to one's inmost self from dragons and serpents points to the danger of the newly acquired consciousness being swallowed up again by the instinctive psyche, the unconscious. The lower vertebrates have from earliest times been favorite symbols of the collective psychic substratum, which is localized anatomically in the subcortical centers, the cerebellum and the spinal cord. These organs constitute the snake. Snake-dreams usually occur, therefore, when the conscious mind is deviating from its instinctual basis.[8]

Jung felt that within the sympathetic system of the body one steps into the deeper collective unconscious, where perhaps psyche and matter share each other's nature:

The deeper "layers" of the psyche lose their individual uniqueness as they retreat farther and farther into darkness. "Lower down," that is to say as they approach the autonomous functional systems, they become increasingly collective until they are universalized and extinguished in the body's materiality, i.e., in chemical substances. The body's carbon is simply carbon. Hence "at bottom" the psyche is simply "world."[9]

Reich established seven segments of the body where armoring takes place, segmental contractions at right angles to the flow of energy in the body. In contrast to these focal points of shadow, the seven chakras have for centuries been known as key psychical centers of consciousness. Historically, the chakras have been islands of light in a dark sea, the refuge of those who, through developed skills, sought to move past the body as shadow. As centers of consciousness, we tend, in the words of Harish Johari, to "understand life's situations from the standpoint of the chakra in which we tend to feel more comfortable and identified."[10]

In a series of seminars on the chakras, held in October 1932 in conjunction with Dr. J. W. Hauer, Jung outlined his sense of their significance in relation to his own system of thought.[11] The first chakra, *muladhara*, located in the perineum, relates us to the world. Associated with our sexuality, it also represents our "root-support," or groundedness. Our consciousness here is merely at a place of ego. We are asleep if we move no further. The first chakra represents earth.

The second chakra, *svadhisthana*, representing water and located in the hypogastric plexus and genitals, is the step into the unconscious, the ocean where the leviathan lives, where one must wrestle in a hero's battle, like Beowulf struggling in the depths of the waters with Grendel's mother. The fight with the monster may bring annihilation, but it also represents a baptism, a source of regeneration after the destruction of the old way. The sun myth is a baptismal story. The sun in the afternoon is old and weak and therefore dies, descending into the western sea, where it travels through the night sea journey until its rebirth on the eastern horizon. The journey into the unconscious is only possible if one has aroused the great serpent, kundalini, which will only be stirred by the correct attitude. Since the journey is long and dangerous, trivial commitments will not do. We must be driven powerfully into the deep; otherwise we would run away. Psychologically, kundalini is what makes us embark on the great adventures. If the knight risks his life for the lady, then the lady is the kundalini. The second chakra is the womb of rebirth and is intensely feminine.

As the sun emerges and its rosy fingers are seen at dawn like jewels in the sky, the third center is reached, the *manipura*, representing fire and emotions, localized in the solar plexus. After the unleashing of the whole emotional world of sex and power, a person must emerge on fire and represent the divine. Anyone who cannot come alive, be impassioned, on fire, is a mere shadow, a washout. In the solar plexus it is well that one is alive and on fire, because there is no freedom there, no air, only bone and muscle and blood and intestines. One is like a worm. To emerge from that unconsciousness is to reach finally the surface of the earth, marked by the diaphragm.

One next reaches the fourth center, the *anahata*, or heart, and the fourth element, air, represented by the lungs, which take in and expel energy—relating the inner and outer worlds. The breath of life is our connection to the Divine Spirit that touches us all across the planet and relates us beyond ego to all living things. One has lifted above the earth finally, and in *anahata* individuation begins. Individuation is the process whereby we become centered somewhere other than in our ego. The ego is found in the first chakra, where we ground with the earth, the *muladhara*, and the self is found in the heart. Crossing the diaphragm brings us from the visible to the invisible, intangible, psychical things. From the heart, thought and feeling are joined. One recognizes values. We reach a level of civilization and personal development. There we come to know the power of psychic phenomena. At the heart level, we come to know that we are contained by something greater than ourselves, which has an entirely psychical existence.

At the fifth level, the *visuddha*, or throat, one comes to know that psychical essences are the fundamental essences of the world. Here we learn to own the projections that we place out on the world, that our worst enemy is merely the vehicle for the projection of ourselves.

In the sixth center, the *ajna*, or third eye, the god who slept in *muladhara* is fully awake, and the psyche, the winged seed, is able to fly. That is, the intuitive function has awakened and sees the images and energy that govern our lives.

The seventh center, the *sahasrara*, or crown chakra, is represented by the lotus of the thousand petals. We reach here our final doorway into enlightenment. The crown chakra is the gateway to another dimension of reality, to our connection with what is durable and eternal, and to the mystical experience of adepts who have preceded us through the centuries. Because of the advancement that knowledge of this level represents, and also because of the untranslatable experiences reported—experiences of nothingness, for instance—we are reduced to general terms and to silence.

The chakras provide images outside of twentieth-century biology, images of enormous power and uncanny accuracy that act upon us. The serpent of divine life uncoils in the dark pelvis of our unconscious and moves through the lotus centers connecting the darkness and light, our unconscious and our awakened state. All the gods, goddesses, and devils are within us, and our bodies open into the cosmos.

In 1933, Heinrich Zimmer, a professor of Indology, spoke on Tantric Yoga at the first Eranos conference, at which Jung also presented a paper.[12] Zimmer stated at that conference:

> All the gods are in our body; nothing else is meant by the visual schema of the Kundalini Yoga, whose adept guides the world-unfolding, world-bearing life-serpent of the macrocosm out of its slumber in the depths, up through the whole body to its suprater-

restrial opposite. On its upward path it passes through the lotus centers of the body, in which all the elements, the material from which the form-hungry vital force makes every form and every gesture, are gathered together, and in the same centers the apparitional forms of the godhead, along with the facets of their *shaktis* [female power], are seen and worshiped.[13]

Body awareness and spiritual awakening have entertained an unnatural separation in the West. Attention to the psychic image and the body's energetic flow open the way to an enlightened, embodied being. Image and energy are the restless vanguard of our being, leading us in and out of shadow.

The limitations that we have accepted by being embodied on the planet are harsh and frustrating. For many the shadows lengthen and overwhelm them with age. Some see these limitations as justifications to avoid the body experience through denial, numbness, or physical aids such as drugs and alcohol. Limitations embitter us at times. Brain injuries or crippling illnesses defy us to find a meaning or purpose in life; and yet, within the psyche of each of us is the winged seed of our enlightenment. There is no problem without solution, no event without purpose for us. The larger self stays hidden and discloses its truths when the ground of our being is fully prepared.

The body is our school, our lesson, our protagonist, our beloved enemy, our shadow and anima/us, the deep friend of our soul. Our bodies, so much the stuff of the world, so sensitive to our inner images, are more changeable than we think, more fluid and spiritual, more infused with light than we guess. Our bodies finally become the jumping-off place into the higher realms, and may accompany us in some higher form into other worlds. We may not be buried with our spears, servants, and favored animals, but if our life continues at the death of the body, some fabric of body may dress us still in a primal and gracious form.

Notes

1. Rainer Maria Rilke, "The Panther," in *Selected Poems of R. M. Rilke,* trans. Robert Bly (New York: Harper & Row, 1983), p. 139.

2. William Blake, "A Memorable Fancy," in *Poems and Letters*, ed. J. Bronowski (Middlesex, England: Penguin, 1986), p. 101.

3. Ibid., p. 102.

4. William Blake, "Proverbs of Hell," in *Poems and Letters*, ed. J. Bronowski (Middlesex, England: Penguin, 1986), p. 96.

5. C. G. Jung, *The Archetypes and the Collective Unconscious*, trans. R. F. C. Hull, ed. Sir Herbert Read, Michael Fordham, and Gerhard Adler, Bollingen Series XX, vol. 9 (Princeton: Princeton University Press, 1980), p. 173.

6. Ibid.

7. C. G. Jung, *The Structure and Dynamics of the Psyche*, 2nd ed., trans. R. F. C. Hull, Bollingen Series XX, vol. 8 (Princeton: Princeton University Press, 1969), p. 326.

8. Jung, *Archetypes*, p. 166.

9. Ibid., p. 173.

10. Harish Johari, *Chakras: Energy Centers of Transformation* (Rochester, Vt.: Destiny Books, 1987), p. 14.

11. C. G. Jung, "Psychological Commentary on Kundalini Yoga," *Spring 1975* (1975): 1–32.

12. The yearly Eranos conferences, organized by Olga Fröbe-Kapteyn, a Dutch theosophist, at her villa on the shore of Lake Maggiore in Italy each August, sought to mediate between Eastern and Western spiritual and psychological traditions. These conferences, in which Jung took a dominant role, brought many brilliant men and women together.

13. Heinrich Zimmer, "The Significance of Tantric Yoga," in *Spiritual Disciplines: Papers from the Eranos Yearbooks*, ed. Joseph Campbell, Bollingen Series XXX, vol. 4 (Princeton: Princeton University Press, 1985), p. 32.

Chapter 15

Image and Energy

Technique has no meaning apart from some informing vision.

—William Barrett

Sexuality is a bond we have with the intimate movement of life, a biological rainbow connecting us to the energetic
heart of nature, to Pan, and to the dark, rich earth. Resting on the
belly of our mother, we take her rhythm of breathing as our own.
When in time we see the rainbow in the sky after a drenching
rain, we are bound by another contract to an awakening Self, and
we are possessed by a flood of unexpected images that determine
our present and future. Whether or not we follow the rainbow of
earth and sky, we come upon our living being, a blend of shadow
and light, energy and image. Reluctantly, we are brought to engage
in elements of our nature that we previously denied were there.
Together, Jung and Reich effectively exposed our denied elements
of spirit and body.

The symbolic and the energetic processes are profoundly
related. We experience the psyche in its outpouring of images, and
the body we experience through the flow and interruption of
energy. Images are to the psyche what energy is to the body; they
form a functional identity.

Bioenergetics and Reichian work have had an implicit ap-
preciation for the underlying image that, caught like a fish in a
net of muscular contraction, embodies the experience of earlier
trauma. The character work that Reich pioneered and Lowen developed identifies the specific childhood injury with the armored
character of the body. Lowen's five styles of character armor tell a

191

story of childhood violation and defense desperately attained through some vital, personal loss of body functioning, a shutting down or reduction of energy to some part of the body. Character analysis investigates the myth or cluster of images underlying the armored body process. Often, however, under financial contraints that limit time, the rigorous study of the body's energy leaves the subtle and ambivalent images unaddressed.

The Jungians, on the other hand, address images and symbols of the psyche through dream analysis and active imagination. In a profound, unexpected way, images bind and release energy. However, not addressing the body directly, the Jungian analyst may override the body's outcry or fail to liberate energy from the body's core. An energetic and (to coin a phrase) "imagetic" approach, attending to bioenergy and bio-image, bridges the mind/body split. Bioenergetics, which stands like Hermes on the borders between the body and the psyche, provides a significant meeting place—or inclusive discipline—for the study of images that inform the energetic process. In this final chapter, I will, as a bioenergetic analyst, explore a few ways in which image and energy, the separate spheres of Jung and Reich, can function together.

From the Jungian viewpoint, the marriage with the Reichian system is a revelation. The shadow is physically revealed. What we have had such difficulty in gaining access to stands blatantly before us in the body. We are given the most direct access to what has been rejected and inaccessible. The masculine and feminine elements, the animus and anima, elusive in dreams, may dance before our eyes, tangibly apparent. Often, our body, reluctant to manifest our contrasexual image in an obvious way, unconsciously seeks out the body of others to hold the image for us. A feminine image that has found no acknowledged expression in our body may draw us to a woman who holds the projection for us. Part of our imagetic work is to observe that contrasexual image in our own body as a parallel to owning our projections.

In the body as shadow, we deal with a body category more inclusive than the armored body: it is the unexpressed, primitive, undifferentiated body; the body lost in darkness. Not merely held back, contracted, or denied, it is a body that reminds us of Michelangelo's "unfinished" sculptures, in which man appears to struggle against the inchoate stone. If an area of the body is cut off from energy and shows no evidence of conflict, it is most likely to have remained undifferentiated, which will be reflected in the underlying shadow images. We are dealing here with a body that needs to be related to but that has lost any conscious relation to itself. In shadow is the body of our family, which may unconsciously determine us. Our mother's walk or our father's bent shoulders may have overcome our own undeveloped disposition. We must physically and psychologically individuate past the family body and liberate our inheritance. The shadow body needs to develop a vocabulary of movement that leads us from the restricted, isolated self-reference to a genuine contact with the world. Armor as an outworn defense must be shaken loose, while the shadow must be related to and owned. By exploring a sequence of movements, a client can be led nonverbally from a body in shadow to a liberated body that stands convincingly in the world.

Often we are caught between our shadow body image, which may seem to us, for instance, to be overweight and ugly, and our ideal body image, which can only be attained by continuous, rigorous dieting and physical training. The swing between these opposites promotes a cynical despair. In a futile gesture, we try to overcome or deny the shadow body. The shadow body often contains images of our sexual and contrasexual self that we are frightened of and wish to defeat. These unrecognized shadow elements hold a power and a breadth of humanity that we cannot afford to lose, even though we lack the courage and understanding to fully accept them. The ideal body image may support us in our shaky image of masculinity or femininity, but at far too great a price. The struggle must be dealt with on the level of internal images. Often our internal images are a rat's nest of misunderstood and misperceived messages from the past, in glaring contradiction to the way others perceive us in the present.

Before the shadow body can be reclaimed, we may need to sort through the shadow images and more specifically identify and distinguish our male and female nature. Armor is often utilized to deny or overcome the contrasexual self. The liberated body is a saner goal than the ideal body, which is often no more than a collection of impersonal cultural stereotypes. We must find images to promote our liberation and let go of images that promote the ideal

body. The liberated body is graceful because it is no longer strain-
ing after an external appearance but represents the acceptance of
shadow elements and a liberation from their unconscious domination. We should appreciate our shadow body. Narcissus could not
see his shadow image, and therefore he drowned in it.

On a physical level, I may have a client stand, as it were, in
his shadow body. I then direct him to stand in his ideal body.
After consciously anchoring these bodily attitudes, I direct him to
design a series of movements that lead him from his shadow body
to his ideal body. This process gives him a certain tangible mastery over the images that have unconsciously determined him, and
it provides me with an abundance of physical and psychological
observations. The client must attend to his determining bio-images.
Later I invite the client to explore a series of movements that lead
toward his liberation. Often through bioenergetic work the bio-
image becomes a felt image, kinesthetically remembered and experienced. The transition to a felt image provides the client with a
way of mastering the determining image and bringing it to full
consciousness.

One of my clients, "George," was ridiculed as a child, and his
sensitivity was discounted as weakness. He was isolated and
rejected by his father, who denied his own feminine side. Later,
George felt that he was not only a "sissy" but "perverted." Against
these devastating images he built an armor. His face and body
became flattened and hard, his eyes narrow, evasive windows in a
besieged fortress, his humor ironic and bitter. My direct work on
the body armor was easily interpreted as an assault and provoked
the armor into a silent resistance. On the other hand, verbally
reaching into the shadow image (the "sissy," the "pervert")—
having that evoked, acknowledged, and brought forward—loos-
ened the armor that was erected partially in denial. George's
friends tended to be people who were extroverted, and their image
completed him, compensated for his withdrawal. It became important for him to incorporate their extroverted image actively and
consciously.

In one exercise, I had George stand in his shadow body, and
then I asked him to develop a few movements that would lead
him into a more liberated body. He did not as yet have a physical
image of liberation. He stood poised on his heels, pulled back,

taut; his eyes, not engaging me, shifted to the left. His next movement brought his weight forward, a fist plunged forward, and he yelled—a karate movement. Then he brought his feet even and opened his arms wide. His heart and face opened. His lower body was not yet truly engaged, but the dance had begun.

Images are a universal language. Some people have the ability to communicate images through an inner clarity of intention that goes beyond words. Traveling in Italy, my wife and I asked an Italian woman in English for directions. Without knowing English, she gave us directions in Italian, and we understood without knowing Italian. There was something involved here that was more than body gestures or words with common roots. Somehow or other, we "caught" her images. But most of us are a contradiction of images, and we lack the simplicity of consonant expression. A guest staying in a second-story bedroom of our house while we were on vacation recalled being unaccountably drawn to looking out the window into the backyard. Then he saw two determined cats staring fixedly at his window. He had forgotten to feed them. Animals, like young children, may communicate directly through image, and, provided with a receptive audience, their basic intentions can be known. As a therapist, I ask myself what the image is behind the slumped shoulder. Is it a shadow image? An armored image? An imitation of an ideal image? Not only must the energy of the body be liberated, but also the image that gives soul to the body's expression.

Often we must address the underlying image directly. Perhaps the image best-suited to awaken our bodies to a lighter, freer form is one from the mythology of our culture—a compelling personality in a film, for example. Just as children model themselves after heroes and heroines, we adults also create our bodies daily according to the image we hold. After we achieve adulthood physically, we seem to be surprised that our body changes at all. Our age comes upon us unexpectedly, unresisted in our ignorance. We expect injury, disease, and incapacity with age, and in this way we assist in our decline. The most coherent image may be mistakenly implanted in terror. The body, bogged down in the realm of images, remains somewhat random and meaningless, easily victimized by images of fear.

A major problem with changing and aging is that we have no

vital alternative image. The therapist awakens the imagination. Sometimes a healthy self-image is impossible for a client; the presence of the therapist in long-term therapy becomes the incorporated inner image. The body, in constant adaptation, leans toward the image it assumes to be itself. If the determining image is inappropriate, the therapist must reach that image, interrupt it, and replace it. In one imagetic intervention, a client of mine saw himself as a tall Indian, and that image automatically brought a lengthening of the neck and relaxation about the shoulders. The direct use of hypnosis can be used to uncover bio-images or implant new images of bodily liberation, but more frequently the mere *awareness* of trance states and hypnotic suggestion serves us adequately. Affirmations accompanied or unaccompanied by gestures are a valuable technique to call forward the archetypes and to program new images, while provoking into conscious recall the negative images they are to replace. The repetition of affirmations introduces powerful new images to replace the undesired negative images that we promote unconsciously. A young man whose energy was withdrawn from his genitals and pelvis was asked to say, "I am a man," while stamping his foot. The gesture moved from the petulant, disbelieving protest of a young boy to a man's forceful, angered assertion.

Sometimes a determining image appears in a dream. One of my clients, "Jim," dreamed that he was a robber baron and that, while he was asleep, his servant encased his body in a cocoon of clay, so that he could hardly move when he awoke. Jim felt this as a threat to his life. His body was chubby and undeveloped. The dream powerfully brought forth the image that had determined his embodiment. He had achieved some wealth as a professional and had studiously avoided physical development, a direction his father championed. The dream image was instrumental in leading him to more physical expression.

A 24-year-old woman, "Alice," began bioenergetic analysis in a state of great agitation. She had difficulty in maintaining contact, was restless, and preferred to be in constant movement. I discovered in time that she misused drugs. Over several years, Alice's tension eased, she was able to be in contact, and she stopped her drug use. However, she felt asexual, although she was clearly an attractive woman with sexual energy to some degree present and available. Long-term bioenergetic work brought relaxation and opening in her chest and pelvis, but a significant change came after a session utilizing active imagination with a dream figure. In her dream, a bad girl that she knew was herself (stiletto heels, short tight skirt, despairing, a drug addict, sexual) warns her good sister against leading such a life. The dream suggested that Alice's drug use was not as peripheral as I had assumed. She had returned to drugs and had been ashamed to tell me. Only through the dialogue and gradual integration of this more primitive feminine image was her body energy free to come into a fuller feminine expression. Her sexuality had been bound by the addiction in an unfortunate attempt to resolve Oedipal issues.

Attention to images is one aspect of the Jungian-Reichian therapeutic work; attention to energy is the other. Sometimes it is more important to become a silent witness to the body's movement, standing or lying down, than to probe with words. As one sits beside a reclined client, one might be fishing in a quiet, still lake, attentive to what lies beneath, or observant of what stirs the surface, respectful of the body's language, which should not always be reduced to words. The symbol, which Jung cautioned is untranslatable, is its own sufficient expression; the body's energy, its deep movement and sound, must also be heard and acknowledged for itself. Reich's later work was characterized by his patient, silent attention to the natural movement of the body energy, the free association of the body. Words, he found, disrupted the body's efforts to assert and restore its own healthy rhythms.

With a new client, I like to observe what I call the individual signature of the body, the particular twists and emphatic turns of the body standing before me. I observe its predispositions, its postural set, its inclinations. I attend to its gestures without having to force a meaning. Standing can function as a free association of the body in which moods attack and dissolve as readily as the images that surface to consciousness. The parade of such subtle movements may lead to a far deeper bodily attention as ambivalence and confusion physically resolve in a new alignment through the standing meditation. The complex challenge of standing evokes our earliest struggles with mobility and independence, issues that often remain unresolved. If attentive and uninterrupted in our standing, we may reorganize ourselves into more graceful balance.

Sometimes I ask the standing client to explore movements that bring pleasure to him while I silently observe. I encourage the client to close his eyes for part of the time to bring his attention more fully to his body process. Frequently, the dance that occurs, like the play of children, goes directly to the key issues. Stiffness and inflexibilities are apparent to the client and the observer-therapist. The restricted vocabulary of movement is readily observable. Pleasure is often experienced in stretching and in expansive movements. The body has its own language, which must be respectfully attended to.

When the client consciously stands in his shadow body and moves toward a liberated body, he creates a dialogue, a bridge of movement into his future, a dance. For instance, there is a tendency in one of my clients for the back of his neck to contract. Like a turtle, he pulls into his body, afraid to stick his neck out, and his chin goes up, creating a small distance of apparent aloofness. The shadow body here reflects withdrawal, neediness, and powerlessness. A small movement of dance is created by the extension of his neck, by the tilt downward of his head; the shoulders lower and the body seeks its own resolution. The client need not try to eradicate his armored distancing posture, and yet he can build a vocabulary of liberation and change from one physical psychic state to another. It is quite alright if at times he feels like withdrawing, because he has the movements that allow choice. The dark instinctual side can take over the body posture without threatening our freedom.

Sometimes childhood conflicts are so brutal and damaging that there is no way through words to escape the psychological prison once it is entered. One client's relationship to her alcoholic mother drew her repeatedly into an unresolvable conflict as an injured child. She also had an image of being a free and effective child, which had developed independently at school. While emotionally she had insufficient resources to climb out of her conflicted state, she developed a sequence of movements that brought her body from the alignment of the shadow body, the conflicted child, to the liberated body of the free child. She could climb out of the conflict on a physical level.

Life as a construct of simple physical rituals can be enacted out of vitality or submerged in depression; and attention to the range of simple human activities is most especially the province of a psychology of the body. As the range of movement is constricted, so our experience is impoverished. Unconsciously locked in the family body, we repeat the gestures and postures of our mother and father and reenact their diseases. Our imaginations and our hearts are designed to extend further than our arms can reach. Whether we like it or not, we are too often contained within a narrow circle of awareness unconsciously restricted by our body's ignorance. We pace the borders of our narrow cage without knowing it. We repeat ourselves gracelessly. If we are to move past the defensive ego, we must explore the body movement that defines us and push more into the potential, our liberated and individuated body.

To gather together the work of Reich and Jung has been no easy task. It is impossible to represent a Reichian technique without neglecting a Jungian alternative. In significant ways, the two men cannot be successfully compared, but stand alone, like great trees commanding their own space and shade. To bring them into a relationship they never enjoyed during their lifetimes may be presumptuous, but to embody their teachings in a dissociated way is equally untenable. We cannot contain them separately, unrelated, any longer. In this chapter, I have suggested one way as a therapist that their work can find harmony under one roof, but their greatness tugs relentlessly at these compromises. While their similarities enliven us, their divergent views of the role of evil, for instance, are deeply disturbing and draw forth a stormy quarrel.

Was Jung right when he saw darkness as an inseparable polarity to light extending from man's inner core of being? The Reichian concept of a genital paradise in the open expression of our core nature keeps us waiting at the gates of heaven, to gain entry through the dissolution of armor and the gift of a pure orgasm reflex. But purity eludes us, and no one can enter a Reichian heaven, not even Reich. Within a few weeks of birth, if not sooner, children have already developed the beginning of armor. Unaffected nature has its grace, but an existential, evolutionary view of the world has welcomed man's fall as the process whereby he was able to develop his consciousness. While a healthy biological spontaneity does give us a glimpse of the Reichian "core nature," such an image becomes an unattained goal in its pure form. The core has value only in dialogue with armor and shadow. Man's liberation is not divorced from the heart of darkness within and around him. Michelangelo's figures, as they struggle out of rock, are not struggling against armor so much as against the unevolved nature, the unlived, unimaged self. There is no nirvana in undeveloped nature, and we need the dialogue with the shadow at our core to individuate. Reich's image of Jesus was of a spontaneous nature in his powerful purity; Reich projected the shadow onto a scheming, uninformed authority who crucified Jesus.

If we relegate the devil to a secondary level, there can be no profound ongoing struggle in our psyche, no alchemy in which we are tried and tested at our core in the fires of hell. With all his deep insights into the underlying life energy of the universe, Reich was nevertheless unable to sufficiently own his shadow, and therefore he was unable to grasp his internal struggle. Instead, he projected his inner struggle outward and had to create his own outer crucifixion. The crucifixion as an image serves us far better as an internal model for the dark night of the soul. At our core, we must be conscious and have choice. Encouraging the spontaneous upsurging of nature, the unblocking of nature's irrepressible life in our bodies, does not provide the sole, ultimate answer.

In fantasy, we would all have better orgasms and a more stressfree life, perhaps in a bucolic setting. Tahiti might bring us more completely in contact with our embodied life, but our creative life might not be served. Writing books placed Reich under tensions that would not have been there had he abandoned the projects for an ideal of bodily bliss. Reich did not live a naive vision, nor did he intend to have his work oversimplified. He knew that to come into wholeness, one faces hell. Physical illness, rather than representing blatant failure, may be a sign of how far we have evolved as we are tested once more in the fire at the core of our lives. Our growth leads us to disclose our injury, and the uncovering of pain may be accompanied by great physical imbalance. Reichian process makes sense as part of an ongoing struggle within the light and shadow at our core. Nevertheless, the question of whether darkness follows us into our deepest center of being is not easily resolved in favor of Jung. Reich had a knowledge of innocence and health, of an unpretentious, natural godliness and purity that presumably Jesus understood. Reich had faith in the children of the future. In his belief in a loving, healthy core exemplified by Jesus, he supported the Christian teaching that proclaims that light exists separately from and free of darkness, a truly revolutionary vision passed on from Jesus. The author of the First Epistle of John wrote: "Here is the message we heard from him [Jesus] and pass on to you; that god is light, and in him there is no darkness at all" (1 John 1:5).

We sustain an evolving consciousness by our vigilance, by our ongoing dialogue with our shadows and all the many voices and images that challenge us, and by clarifying our images and energy. At the deepest levels, we must have meaning and intention; otherwise we sink into determining images that unconsciously direct us, images that by nature are not always benign. Without clarified intentions and positive images of embodiment, we are powerlessly swept up in collective actions, our futile hopes scrawled on paper in a bottle tossed out at sea.

Bibliography

Andersen, Hans Christian. "The Shadow." In *Hans Christian Andersen: Eighty Fairytales*. New York: Pantheon Press, 1982.

Andreas-Salomé, Lou. *The Freud Journal of Lou Andreas-Salomé*. Trans. Stanley A. Leavy. New York: Basic Books, 1964.

Bertin, Celia. *Marie Bonaparte: A Life*. New York: Harcourt Brace Jovanovich, 1982.

Bettelheim, Bruno. "Scandal in the Family." *New York Review of Books*, 30 (June 30, 1983): 39.

Blake, William. *Poems and Letters*. Ed. J. Bronowski. Middlesex, England: Penguin, 1986.

Brome, Vincent. *Jung: Man and Myth*. New York: Atheneum, 1978.

Bunyan, John. *The Pilgrim's Progress*. Ed. Roger Shamrock. Harmondsworth, England: Penguin, 1965.

Capra, Fritjof. *The Tao of Physics*. New York: Bantam, 1976.

Carotenuto, Aldo. *A Secret Symmetry: Sabina Spielrein Between Jung and Freud*. Trans. Arno Pomerans, John Shepley, and Krishna Winston. New York: Pantheon, 1982.

Dante Alighieri. *The Inferno*. Trans. John Ciardi. New York: Mentor, 1954.

Doolittle, Hilda. *Tribute to Freud*. New York: New Directions, 1974.

Fordham, Michael, ed. *Contact with Jung*. Philadelphia: Lippincott, 1963.

Franz, Marie-Louise von. *Alchemy: An Introduction to the Symbolism and the Psychology*. Ed. Daryl Sharp. Toronto: Inner City Books, 1980.

_____. *Shadow and Evil in Fairytales*. Zurich: Spring Publications, 1974.

Freeman, Derek. *Margaret Mead and Samoa: The Making and Unmaking of an Anthropological Myth*. Cambridge, Mass.: Harvard University Press, 1983.

Freud, Sigmund. *Collected Papers*. 5 vols. London: Hogarth Press, 1950.

_____. *Origins of Psychoanalysis: Letters to Wilhelm Fliess, Drafts and Notes, 1887–1902*. Ed. Marie Bonaparte, Anna Freud, and Ernst Kris. Trans. Eric Mosbacher and James Strachey. New York: Basic Books, 1954.

_____. *The Problem of Anxiety*. Trans. Henry Alden Bunker, M.D. New York: W. W. Norton, 1936.

Hannah, Barbara. *Jung: His Life and Work—A Biographical Memoir*. New York: Putnam's, 1976.

Henderson, Joseph L. "C. G. Jung: A Personal Evaluation." In *Contact with Jung*, ed. Michael Fordham. Philadelphia: Lippincott, 1963.

I Ching or Book of Changes, The. Trans. Richard Wilhelm and Cary F. Baynes. Bollingen Series XIX. Princeton: Princeton University Press, 1967.

Jacoby, Russell. *The Repression of Psychoanalysis: Otto Fenichel and the Political Freudians*. New York: Basic Books, 1983.

Johari, Harish. *Chakras: Energy Centers of Transformation*. Rochester, Vt.: Destiny Books, 1987.

Jung, C. G. *AION: Researches into the Phenomenology of the Self*. 2nd ed. Trans. R. F. C. Hull. Bollingen Series XX, vol. 9. Princeton: Princeton University Press, 1968.

_____. *Alchemical Studies*. Trans. R. F. C. Hull. Bollingen Series XX, vol. 13. Princeton: Princeton University Press, 1967.

_____. *Analytical Psychology: Its Theory and Practice*. New York: Vintage, 1968.

_____. *The Answer to Job*. Trans. R. F. C. Hull. Bollingen Series XX, vol. 11. Princeton: Princeton University Press, 1973.

_____. *The Archetypes and the Collective Unconscious*. Trans. R. F. C. Hull. Ed. Sir Herbert Read, Michael Fordham, and Gerhard Adler. Bollingen Series XX, vol. 9. Princeton: Princeton University Press, 1980.

_____. *C. G. Jung Letters*. 2 vols. Trans. R. F. C. Hull. Ed. Gerhard Adler and Aniela Jaffé. Bollingen Series XCV. Princeton: Princeton University Press, 1973.

_____. *Civilization in Transition*. 2nd ed. Trans. R. F. C. Hull. Bollingen Series XX, vol. 10. Princeton: Princeton University Press, 1970.

_____. *Flying Saucers: A Myth of Things Seen in the Skies*. Trans. R. F. C. Hull. Bollingen Series XX, vol. 10. Princeton: Princeton University Press, 1978.

_____. *Four Archetypes: Mother/Rebirth/Spirit/Trickster*. Trans. R. F. C. Hull. Bollingen Series XX, vol. 9. Princeton: Princeton University Press, 1970.

_____. *Memories, Dreams, Reflections*. Rev. ed. Trans. Richard and Clara Winston. Ed. Aniela Jaffé. New York: Pantheon, 1973.

_____. *Modern Man in Search of a Soul*. Trans. W. S. Dell and Cary F. Baynes. New York: Harvest, 1933.

_____. *Mysterium Coniunctionis: An Inquiry into the Separation and Synthesis of Psychic Opposites in Alchemy*. 2nd ed. Trans. R. F. C. Hull. Bollingen Series XX, vol. 14. Princeton: Princeton University Press, 1977.

_____. *The Practice of Psychotherapy: Essays on the Psychology of the Transference and Other Subjects*. 2nd ed. Trans. R. F. C. Hull. Bollingen Series XX, vol. 16. Princeton: Princeton University Press, 1966.

_____. *The Psychogenesis of Mental Disease*. Trans. R. F. C. Hull. Bollingen Series XX, vol. 3. Princeton: Princeton University Press, 1960.

_____. "Psychological Commentary on Kundalini Yoga." *Spring 1975* (1975): 1–32.

_____. *Psychological Types.* Trans. H. G. Baynes. Ed. R. F. C. Hull. Bollingen Series XX, vol. 6. Princeton: Princeton University Press, 1976.

_____. *Psychology and Alchemy.* Bollingen Series XX, vol. 12. Princeton: Princeton University Press, 1977.

_____. *The Psychology of the Transference.* Bollingen Series XX, vol. 16. Princeton: Princeton University Press, 1974.

_____. "A Seminar with C. G. Jung: Comments on a Child's Dream (1936–37)." *Spring 1974* (1974): 205–206.

_____. *The Structure and Dynamics of the Psyche.* 2nd ed. Trans. R. F. C. Hull. Bollingen Series XX, vol. 8. Princeton: Princeton University Press, 1969.

_____. *Symbols of Transformation: An Analysis of the Prelude to a Case of Schizophrenia.* 2nd ed. Trans. R. F. C. Hull. Bollingen Series XX, vol. 5. Princeton: Princeton University Press, 1956.

_____. *Two Essays on Analytical Psychology.* 2nd ed. Trans. R. F. C. Hull. Bollingen Series XX, vol. 7. Princeton: Princeton University Press, 1972.

_____, and W. Pauli. *The Interpretation of Nature and the Psyche.* New York: Pantheon, 1955.

Keyhoe, Donald. *Flying Saucers from Outer Space.* New York: Henry Holt, 1953.

Lawrence, D. H. *Selected Literary Criticism.* Ed. Anthony Beal. New York: Viking Press, 1956.

McGuire, William, ed. *The Freud/Jung Letters: The Correspondence Between Sigmund Freud and C. G. Jung.* Trans. Ralph Manheim and R. F. C. Hull. Bollingen Series XCIV. Princeton: Princeton University Press, 1974.

_____, and R. F. C. Hull, eds. *C. G. Jung Speaking: Interviews and Encounters.* Bollingen Series XVII. Princeton: Princeton University Press, 1972.

Neumann, Erich. *Creative Man: Five Essays: Kafka/Trakl/Chagall/Freud/Jung.* Trans. Eugene Rolfe. Bollingen Series LXI, vol. 2. Princeton: Princeton University Press, 1982.

_____. "Mystical Man." Trans. Ralph Manheim. *Spring 1961* (1961): 9–49.

Oakes, Maud. *The Stone Speaks: The Memoir of a Personal Transformation.* Wilmette, Ill.: Chiron Publications, 1987.

Pfeiffer, Ernst, ed. *Sigmund Freud and Lou Andreas-Salomé: Letters.* Trans. William and Elaine Robson-Scott. New York: W. W. Norton, 1985.

Ranade, R. D. *Mysticism in India: The Poet-Saints of Maharashtra.* Albany, N.Y.: State University of New York Press, 1983.

Rank, Otto. *Beyond Psychology*. New York: Dover, 1941.

_____. "Der Doppelgänger." *Imago*, 3 (1914): 97–164.

_____. *The Double: A Psychoanalytic Study*. Trans. and ed. Harry Tucker, Jr. New York: Meridian, 1971.

Ravenscroft, Trevor. *The Spear of Destiny*. New York: Putnam's, 1973.

Reich, Ilse Ollendorff. *Wilhelm Reich: A Personal Biography*. New York: St. Martin's Press, 1969.

Reich, Peter. *A Book of Dreams*. Greenwich, Ct.: Fawcett, 1973.

Reich, Wilhelm. *The Bion Experiments on the Origin of Life*. Trans. Derek and Inge Jordan. Ed. Mary Higgins and Chester M. Raphael. New York: Octagon, 1979.

_____. *The Cancer Biopathy* (vol. 2 of *The Discovery of the Orgone*). Trans. Andrew White with Mary Higgins and Chester M. Raphael. New York: Farrar, Straus, & Giroux, 1973.

_____. *Character Analysis*. 3rd ed. Trans. Theodore P. Wolfe. New York: Farrar, Straus & Giroux, 1949.

_____. *Cosmic Superimposition*. Trans. Mary Boyd Higgins and Therese Pol. New York: Farrar, Straus & Giroux, 1973.

_____. *Ether, God, and Devil*. Trans. Mary Boyd Higgins and Therese Pol. New York: Farrar, Straus & Giroux, 1973.

_____. *The Function of the Orgasm*. Trans. Theodore P. Wolfe. New York: Meridian, 1970.

_____. *Genitality in the Theory and Therapy of Neurosis*. 2nd ed. Trans. Philip Schmitz. Ed. Mary Higgins and Chester M. Raphael. New York: Farrar, Straus & Giroux, 1980.

_____. *The Impulsive Character and Other Writings*. Trans. Barbara G. Koopman. New York: New American Library, 1974.

_____. *Listen, Little Man!* Trans. Ralph Manheim. New York: Farrar, Straus & Giroux, 1974.

_____. *The Mass Psychology of Fascism*. Trans. Vincent R. Carfagno. New York: Farrar, Straus & Giroux, 1970.

_____. *The Murder of Christ* (vol. 1 of *The Emotional Plague of Mankind*). New York: Simon & Schuster, 1953.

_____. *Passion of Youth: An Autobiography, 1897–1922*. Ed. Mary Boyd Higgins and Chester M. Raphael, with translations by Philip Schmitz and Jerri Tompkins. New York: Farrar, Straus & Giroux, 1988.

_____. *People in Trouble* (vol. 2 of *The Emotional Plague of Mankind*). Trans. Philip Schmitz. New York: Farrar, Straus & Giroux, 1976.

_____. *Reich Speaks of Freud*. New York: Farrar, Straus & Giroux, 1967.

_____. *Wilhelm Reich: Early Writings*. Trans. Philip Schmitz. New York: Farrar, Straus & Giroux, 1975. •

Rilke, Rainer Maria. *Selected Poems of R. M. Rilke*. Trans. Robert Bly. New York: Harper & Row, 1983.

Roazen, Paul. *Freud and His Followers*. New York: Mentor, 1974.

Roustang, François. *Dire Mastery: Discipleship from Freud to Lacan*. Trans. Ned Lukacher. Baltimore: Johns Hopkins University Press, 1982.

Sharaf, Myron. *Fury on Earth: A Biography of Wilhelm Reich*. New York: St. Martin's Press, 1983.

Snow, C. P. *The Two Cultures; and A Second Look*. Cambridge, England: Cambridge University Press, 1969.

Stepansky, Paul E. *In Freud's Shadow: Adler in Context*. Hillsdale, N.J.: Analytic Press, 1983.

Sterba, Richard F. *Reminiscences of a Viennese Psychoanalyst*. Detroit: Wayne State University Press, 1982.

Sulloway, Frank J. *Freud: Biologist of the Mind—Beyond the Psychoanalytic Legend*. New York: Basic Books, 1979.

Walker, Mitchell. "The Double: An Archetypal Configuration." *Spring 1976* (1976): 165–175.

Whitman, Walt. *Leaves of Grass*. New York: New American Library, 1958.

Zimmer, Heinrich. "The Significance of Tantric Yoga." In *Spiritual Disciplines: Papers from the Eranos Yearbooks*, ed. Joseph Campbell. Bollingen Series XXX, vol. 4. Princeton: Princeton University Press, 1985.

Index